Praise for *Life, Part Two*

"I have been waiting for this book, and it's as good as I hoped. David Chernikoff distills wisdom from his decades of studying and practicing Buddhism and other contemplative traditions, depicting the wise elderhood that our culture so needs."

—David Loy, author of
Ecodharma: Buddhist Teachings for the Ecological Crisis

"*Life, Part Two* reminds us that there is still time to become the person we were meant to be. David Chernikoff's Buddhist message is exactly what we need at a moment when we are looking for realistic hope for the second half of life."

—Harry R. Moody, author of
Aging: Concepts and Controversies

"Have you considered looking deeply at what life and death are about? In *Life, Part Two*, David Chernikoff shares a world of reflection, contemplation, and curiosity. The book offers insight into life and in turn supports the idea of a peaceful approach to the end of life. Separately, each chapter is a stepping-stone, and all together they show a path to graceful aging and acceptance."

—Sharon Salzberg, author of
ange

D1112921

"Growing older is often seen as something to dread or stoically accept. What if instead of resignation we could approach it with a spirit of adventure, opening to the next chapter of our life with celebration and discovery? *Life, Part Two* gives us a roadmap to do just that. As a leading teacher in the field of conscious aging, David Chernikoff has synthesized a lifetime exploring wisdom teachings into his own profound recipe for aging gracefully. Filled with engaging stories, including his personal journey, Chernikoff shows how to not just get through this stage of life but to thrive in the process."

—James Baraz, author of
Awakening Joy: 10 Steps to Happiness

LIFE, PART TWO

SEVEN KEYS TO AWAKENING WITH PURPOSE AND JOY AS YOU AGE

David Chernikoff

Shambhala Publications, Inc.
2129 13th Street
Boulder, Colorado 80302
www.shambhala.com

© 2021 by David Chernikoff

Cover art: franckreporter/iStock
Cover design: Daniel Urban-Brown
Interior design: Gopa & Ted2, Inc

9 8 7 6 5 4 3 2 1

First Edition
Printed in the United States of America

⊛ This edition is printed on acid-free paper that meets
the American National Standards Institute z39.48 Standard.
♻ Shambhala Publications makes every effort to print on
recycled paper. For more information please visit
www.shambhala.com.
Shambhala Publications is distributed worldwide by
Penguin Random House, Inc., and its subsidiaries.

Library of Congress Cataloging-in-Publication Data
Names: Chernikoff, David (David Barry), author.
Title: Life, part two: seven keys to awakening with purpose
and joy as you age / David Chernikoff.
Description: First edition. | Boulder, Colorado: Shambhala, [2021] |
Includes bibliographical references.
Identifiers: LCCN 2021016345 | ISBN 9781611808612 (paperback)
Subjects: LCSH: Aging—Psychological aspects. | Aging—Religious
aspects. | Self-actualization (Psychology) in middle age. |
Self-actualization (Psychology) in old age. | Consciousness. |
Consciousness—Religious aspects. | Spiritual life.
Classification: LCC BF724.55.A35 C44 2021 | DDC 155.67—dc23
LC record available at https://lccn.loc.gov/2021016345

CONTENTS

INTRODUCTION

REB ZALMAN was seventy-two years old when I met him in 1996. I had known about him for many years before we met in person. He was a much-loved and somewhat controversial spiritual teacher who embodied authentic loving-kindness, deep wisdom, and incredible chutzpah. I met him shortly after he came to Naropa University as a recipient of the World Wisdom Chair, a recently endowed position in the religious studies department. At the time I was in my mid-forties and teaching meditation and psychology in the Transpersonal Psychology graduate program at Naropa.[1]

One of the benefits Naropa faculty members received at that time was the opportunity to take as many course credits as we taught without having to pay for the classes. When I heard that Reb Zalman was offering a course called "Rituals for People Helpers," I immediately signed up. I was on a soapbox at the time in relation to how completely our society had dispensed with meaningful rites of passage and other rituals designed to mark the passing of our lives. In our zeal to create a secular, scientific worldview, I felt strongly that we had gone too far and largely lost touch with the inherent sacredness of life.

The course, held at a local Unitarian Universalist church, was very much what I was looking for, and Reb Zalman was every bit as charismatic and engaging as I'd been told he would be. After the second class, I spoke to his assistant and arranged to meet with him individually. I wasn't exactly sure why I wanted to meet with Reb Zalman. Something deep beneath the surface of my awareness was operating, and I was granted only a very occasional glimpse of it before it once again disappeared like a black cat in the dead of night.

On the appointed day, I stayed after class and met with Reb Zalman in the room he was using as a temporary office at the church. He greeted me warmly as I settled into the chair across from him and began to speak. "I'm not really sure why I wanted to meet with you. I've known about your teachings and your work for quite a while. I worked with two of Ram Dass's organizations at points along the way, and he spoke very highly of you." I paused at that point, unsure how to proceed. Reb Zalman held my gaze without the least sense of being in a hurry. He was completely attentive, and his presence invited me to show up in the same way.

"Here's what's going on," I said, releasing the cautiousness and fear I was struggling with. "My life looks really great from the outside. I'm forty-six years old. I have a wonderful wife and a beautiful five-year-old daughter. I enjoy the classes I teach at Naropa and love the students. My private practice is thriving, and I often have a wait list.

I'm one of the guiding teachers for the Insight Meditation Community of Colorado. All of these activities represent long-held aspirations that I've been blessed to be able to bring to fruition in my life."

I looked up, and Reb Zalman had an expression of curiosity on his face. His whole body seemed to be saying, "And . . . what led you to want to see me?"

"The problem is," I continued, "I'm dying on the inside. I'm too busy, carrying too much emotional responsibility, and feeling hooked on being a helper and a 'good guy.' All of these people are coming to me with outstretched arms, both literally and figuratively. They seem to be looking for the good father, for the unconditional love they didn't experience at earlier points along the way. It's way too much for me to carry. Who am *I* supposed to turn to? Who is supposed to support *me?* I guess that's why I'm here. I need a mentor. I need help myself, from someone who recognizes that I have challenges and difficulties, too. I think I'm here to ask you to be a mentor to me. Someone who can teach me to live a balanced life, a life in which I care for others and also care for my family and for myself. Yes, I think that's why I'm here."

Reb Zalman hadn't said a word since I began my Woody Allen-esque monologue. When I stopped, he smiled in a way that felt like sunshine emerging from behind a cloud. After a brief pause, he said, "That's perfect. You be the papa. I'll be the grandpa. I'll take you on."

I felt stunned at first, unsure of the implications of what he was saying. At the same time, the whole situation felt so completely right. I savored the moment and took in the brilliant light and warmth of his love. Clearly, *that* was what I had come for.

For those of us who feel deeply committed to spiritual realization and to being instruments of benefit in the world, what Carl Jung called "the second half of life" represents a remarkable curriculum for awakening.[2] The challenges inherent in the aging process can become a direct pathway to the actualization of our best human qualities—wisdom, joy, compassion, generosity, lovingkindness, and equanimity. Although I didn't know it that day, this was precisely the possibility I began glimpsing in my first meeting with Reb Zalman. His way of embracing and enjoying the role of wise elder planted a seed of transformation that helped me to relate to the aging process in a new and life-affirming way, and it's one that's been growing ever since.

A week after our initial meeting, he called me and invited me to join the board of directors of what was then called the Spiritual Eldering Institute (now Sage-ing International). This conscious aging organization offered educational programs for the general public and professional trainings for people who wanted to become Certified Sage-ing Leaders (CSLs). I was very moved by the work the institute was doing, and I decided to go through the professional training program so I could share Reb Zalman's work with others. About eighteen months after I completed the program and had been teaching the material for a while, I was hired to be the institute's director of education and training.

What moved me about the work of the institute was its recognition of how much unnecessary suffering people in our modern Western society experience because of our unwise understanding of the aging process. It is a classic example of a kind of adventitious suffering rooted in our collective belief system about what it means to become an elderly human being. As a gifted and prophetic visionary, Reb Zalman called for nothing less than a paradigm shift in regard to our society's dominant model of growing old.

His views on aging arose in part out of a depression he experienced as he approached his sixtieth birthday. While on one level he had been remarkably productive and beneficial to others throughout much of his life, he was aware of a sinking feeling that he was on the verge of being seen as over the hill in the eyes of society. He could feel the deeply conditioned negative beliefs and attitudes he had absorbed from Western culture with its loud, frequent messages that youthfulness is desirable, and old age is to be dreaded as a time when a person gets cast aside like a worn shoe. Worse yet, because of the size of the baby boom generation, so-called senior citizens are frequently seen as a burden to their families and a drain on the economy, further eroding their self-esteem. Reb Zalman pointed out what many of us knew to be true: In wise, indigenous cultures, the elders were (and are) highly respected for their maturity and life experience. They are understood to be lineage holders and repositories of wisdom.

The work I did with Reb Zalman and the Spiritual Eldering Institute brought manifold blessings into my life. It had numerous parallels to hospice work I had done in my late twenties and early to mid-thirties. In the same way that our culture's denial of death leads to insensitive and uncompassionate ways of dealing with human beings at the end of their lives, confused thinking leads people who are getting older—approaching a fiftieth birthday, a sixtieth, or whatever age subjectively resonates for an individual—to believe they are past their prime, soon to be of little use to their families and society. Because of the power of self-fulfilling prophecy—something that social scientists have long recognized—those of us who unconsciously absorb the distorted views of aging that our culture embraces are at high risk of creating just the kind of elderhood we fear most.

This sad truth has been supported by research in the field of social and personality psychology. One clinical study pointed out what many of us intuitively know to be true. The researchers concluded that "older individuals with more positive self-perceptions of aging, measured up to 23 years earlier, lived 7.5 years longer than those with less positive self-perceptions of aging. This advantage remained after age, gender, socioeconomic status, loneliness, and functional health were included as covariates."[3] In other words, our *beliefs* about aging, in and of themselves, influence our quality of life and our longevity in a significant way. If someone invented a pharmaceutical drug that had no negative side effects and would enable us to live 7.5 years longer, it would be announced by a two-inch headline in the *New York Times*. Needless to say, the results of this study did not receive much attention from the popular press or have any real impact on our society's pernicious attitudes toward elders.

Jung's use of the phrase "second half of life" emphasizes the chronological aspect of the aging process. There's another meaning associated with this phrase, one that is not as well understood in Western society. I've noticed in my own life and in my work with others that the process of spiritual maturation regularly requires us to let go of our familiar psychological identity and our customary view of reality so we can see ourselves and the world with fresh eyes. This is a kind of ego-death, which can occur for a person of any age, and it reveals an additional meaning of the phrase "second half of life." For one person, this might involve life before and after a cancer diagnosis. For another, it could be associated with the end of an intimate relationship. For yet another, it might be the result of leaving a long-time career to start a new one or to retire. There are countless possibilities in this regard, yet they all result in the same "felt sense" that something fundamental has changed. As one person said to me in a life coaching session, "It's more than feeling like I'm in a new chapter. It's that I feel like I'm starting 'book two' of my life."

There's a related saying attributed to the Zen tradition that "those who die before they die are free to really live."

In this case, the first half of life ends when the practitioner experiences a profound breakthrough realization that turns them inside out and upside down. Life is both the same *and* radically different after such an inner event. Similarly, being "born again" in the Christian tradition can be understood in this context as beginning anew, while at the same time building on the life that came before.

This second interpretation was the inspiration of this book's title and makes *Life, Part Two* for anyone who is sincerely committed to looking deeply at what life and death are all about. In the chapters to come, I've combined these two perspectives on the second half of life—sometimes emphasizing the chronological aspect of growing older, and other times including the more general meaning of the phrase that speaks to all people who aspire to awaken in this present life. What's important to recognize is that "conscious aging" and "conscious living" are one and the same process. The former applies to people who are moving through midlife and beyond, while the latter reminds us that we're *all* living, aging, and dying in each moment of our existence.

Recent global events have made it increasingly obvious to me that our world doesn't need more Buddhists, Hindus, Christians, Jews, Muslims, Wiccans, humanists, or atheists. It doesn't need more Democrats, Republicans, or Libertarians either. What it desperately needs is more people who embody and express the qualities mentioned earlier: wisdom, joy, compassion, generosity, lovingkindness, and equanimity. In addition, a pluralistic mindset is urgently needed now so we can effectively address the variety of social, political, religious, and environmental issues that are calling out for wise attention. With this book, I invite you, the reader, to affirm and invigorate your personal path—whether within one religion, as a "multiple-belonger," or as a spiritual-but-not-religious individual. At the same time, I challenge you to become the kind of person that each of us is inherently capable of being, a person who can look seven generations into the future and help to shift our collective trajectory to a more cooperative, life-sustaining direction.

This is an incredibly powerful time to be living on our fragile and beautiful planet. What we human beings need more than anything else is to cultivate a change of heart. If we want to address this critical task, we must renew our commitment to the *core principles* that unite the seemingly diverse approaches to conscious living and dying. Although these principles can be identified in a variety of ways, in this book I've organized them into seven key categories:

- Embracing the mystery
- Choosing a vision
- Awakening intuition
- Committing to inner work
- Suffering effectively
- Serving from the heart
- Celebrating the journey

These sacred skills are most effectively integrated and evident in the role of the wise elder, an archetype that the world's indigenous cultures have long honored and one that we in modern society have largely forgotten. Even so, let's be honest about the fact that living a long time doesn't automatically make a person wise or compassionate. We've all met elders who seem to embody the way we *don't* want to be when we grow old. The focus of this book, however, is on the inner work we can all do that synthesizes wisdom and love from long life experience. I've had the good fortune to learn a great deal from people who have done just that, amazing elders who understood that their very reason for being was to live an awakened life and to leave a clearly visible trail for those who aspire to follow in their footsteps. I give thanks daily for the joy, courage, freedom, and blessings that such people have so generously brought into my life.

Throughout this book, I'll be weaving together personal experiences and insights; teachings I've received from various spiritual guides; and stories shared with me in the intimacy of my work as a meditation teacher, spiritual counselor, life coach, hospice worker, and psychotherapist. To honor confidentiality, I've changed details and created composites of various people in certain stories while doing my best to convey the spirit of what occurred. I've also included poems and quotations that serve to illustrate aspects of the seven keys to awakened living.

I have one request as we begin our safari of the soul together. Whether you're a long-time spiritual practitioner or a novice who received this book as a gift from a caring friend, I ask that you leave your preconceptions about the second half of life here at our initial campsite. You can always pick them up again when we return. Give yourself complete permission to be a learner, suspend your disbelief or cynicism, and be genuinely curious about who you might be and how you might live your life when you complete the pilgrimage we're about to share. Let's be on our way now.

CHAPTER ONE
EMBRACING THE MYSTERY

I live my life in growing orbits,
which move out over the things of the world.
Perhaps I can never achieve the last,
but that will be my attempt.

I am circling around God, around the ancient tower,
and I have been circling for a thousand years.
And I still don't know if I am a falcon,
Or a storm, or a great song.

—RAINER MARIA RILKE

IT STARTED OUT as an ordinary summer day. I spent the better part of August 9, 1963, looking forward to the Little League baseball game I'd be pitching in the evening. At thirteen years old, I was an aspiring Cleveland Indian (now the Cleveland Guardians, as the organization has jettisoned its long use of a race-based name) whose current "career stage" in baseball involved playing shortstop and pitcher for the Oxford Shop, a team sponsored by a clothing store owned by my friend Kenny's father. I rode my bike up to the playing field for the 6:30 P.M. game and thoroughly enjoyed our 9–1 victory over Monarch Electric. After hanging around the field a few minutes to talk to friends and their fathers, I rode my bike home as the darkness settled over the small town of Beachwood, Ohio.

I entered the house through the screened-in back porch that we routinely used to enter and leave. "Hi," I shouted, "I'm home." No answer. That was quite unusual, so I called out again. Still no answer. Then I noticed a note on the kitchen table. It said, "We had to take Daddy to the hospital. Stay home and we'll call you."

I waited, worried, and waited some more. I tried to watch TV, but I couldn't focus on it. An hour later, my uncle Al, who lived with us, came home and told me what had happened. He seemed shaken and distracted, not his usual mellow self. "Your dad had a heart attack," he said. Then there was an awkward pause. I sensed in that moment that something was *very* wrong. "He died a little while ago at Mount Sinai Hospital." I heard the words, but they didn't register. As far as I knew, Daddy wasn't even sick. How could he possibly just die all of a sudden?

Unable to tolerate the emotions that started to surface, I became completely numb and withdrew from everyone. For the next ten days, which included the funeral and the Jewish ritual of sitting shiva, I simply went through the motions. Life seemed like a surreal dream, and I didn't feel one emotion that I can remember.

Three days after the funeral, I was staring blankly at a morning TV show before "the people" started coming over with trays of food, bottles of Jewish wine, and quiet conversation. I heard the front doorbell ring. My mother came to get me and said, "It's Rabbi Levine. He's come over to talk to you." I felt taken aback at first, quite irritated. *Why wasn't I told about this?* I thought to myself. I dutifully walked into the living room, which was only used for "company," and after a mechanical exchange of greetings, my mother invited the rabbi to have a seat and then left the room. I stood there at first, realizing that this had been set up as a time for the rabbi to talk with me about my dad's death. I took a seat across from him. He was a kind man with a good heart and deep blue eyes that seemed sad and lonely to me at that moment.

"How are you doing, son?" he asked.

I felt speechless. "OK," I said. "I guess I'm doing OK."

"I'm sure you've been through a great deal in the last week or so. It takes a long time and a lot of patience to digest a big life change like the death of your father."

I looked down at my hands, unsure how to respond. There were huge, powerful emotions off in the distance like the jet passenger planes that flew over our house from time to time, heading for Cleveland Hopkins Airport. I felt a sudden rush of anger, of outrage, at the unfairness of the situation. With fire in my eyes, I looked at Rabbi Levine and said, "Why my father? He was such a good man!" I remember thinking to myself, *There are all these rotten people out there who deserve to die, and my father dies so suddenly and unexpectedly. Why my father?*

The good rabbi held my gaze without flinching and

became quiet for a moment. "David, son, there are some things that God does that we just don't understand."

I found that comment completely unsatisfactory. I don't remember any of the conversation that followed except that there were long, silent pauses, and I looked down at my hands a lot. We talked for about ten more minutes until my mom came into the room. During one of those pauses, she thanked the rabbi for his visit, I shook his hand, and he left.

At the time of my encounter with the rabbi, I was too young and too grief-stricken to fully grasp the importance of what he was trying to convey to me. But looking back, I can see that there was an essential truth in his response to my question—he was trying to talk to me about the mystery of living and dying. And indeed, for me, spiritual awakening began with the seed of insight planted by Rabbi Levine in our awkward conversation that day in the living room. It took time, yet that seed eventually grew into a deeply felt recognition that the lives we live are filled with and surrounded by an ever-present quality of mystery.

For the first five years after my father's death, I was emotionally numb and withdrawn much of the time. An introvert by nature, I became moody and sullen. My grief and my anger at life were often quite near the surface but had no outlet that felt safe or appropriate. The sense of mystery started to come alive when I entered undergraduate school at Tulane University in 1968. My initial impulse when I saw how little I actually understood about life was to find *the* answer—the Holy Grail, the master key to the secret at the center of Reality. Without even thinking about it, I assumed there had to be an answer and that when I found it, I would be freed from the prison of sadness, fear, anger, and craving I so often experienced when I took an honest look inside my heart. It would be many years before I fully appreciated the truth of a statement made by the religious scholar Huston Smith, who said, "We are born in mystery, we live in mystery, and we die in mystery."[1]

Coming of age in the late 1960s, I tried partying my way to a happier life—and failed miserably. Like so many others of the baby boom generation, I then came to see myself as a "spiritual seeker." Looking back, I can see how deep-seated feelings of inadequacy turned my life into an ongoing self-improvement project. If I practiced enough yoga postures, spent enough hours studying the Bhagavad Gita or the Tao Te Ching, recited enough mantras, dated the right person, ate a healthy enough vegetarian diet, or cultivated sufficient devotion and emotional intelligence, then I would have what I needed to crack the secret code of existence. I would transcend the suffering that so often rained down upon my life and the lives of those around me, both human beings and other living creatures of every kind. I would finally be worthy of love. I can see now how desperately I sought to control what cannot be controlled and to understand the incomprehensible. I can see how much my "need to know" was a need to feel safe, a desire to be invulnerable to the vicissitudes of life. That would protect me from ever again having to experience the shock and heartbreak I felt when my father died.

While this was a very lonely time in my life, I eventually came to see that I was not alone. My undergraduate psychology training made me aware of how many forms of psychological pain human beings experience. The diagnostic manual for mental health professionals, with its near exclusive focus on psychopathology, read like a catalogue of suffering, a seemingly endless list of the emotional, cognitive, and behavioral struggles in the lives of human beings. Perhaps the difficulties in my own life were not *all* the result of my personal hang-ups or my basic badness. Perhaps the human condition was more complex and ungraspable than I had hoped. Perhaps there was an important relationship between what one of my teachers called "*my* pain and *the* pain."

In my work with conscious aging programs, I've noticed that the issue of mystery arises in different ways. The first has to do with one beneficial effect that growing older has on many people. As we move into midlife and then through it into the last third of our lives, many of us recognize that the "secret at the center" continues to be elusive and conclude that it doesn't exist at all. Consciously or unconsciously, we start to understand that the transformation of consciousness is most often a matter of small steps in ordinary circumstances, the proverbial journey of a thousand miles that begins with one step. We discover the sacred mystery present in every moment of our lives. As Buddhist teacher Thich Nhat Hanh put it, "The miracle is not to walk on water. The miracle is to walk on the green earth, dwelling deeply in the present moment and feeling truly alive."[2]

There's also a shadow side to this miraculous mystery that I've observed in my own life and my work with others. For some of us, the pain and struggle that accumulate in our lives lead to desensitization, a numbing and emotional shutdown of the kind I experienced after my father died. Life is so very difficult at times. It's natural for us to tense our muscles, harden our hearts, and disengage from emotions that feel unbearable. It's part of how the wisdom of our bodies protects us. While it's essential that we have compassion for ourselves and each other when we pull back from the rawness of life, it's also important to acknowledge that we may have to actively participate in our own healing to avoid living a "lifeless life," one in which our hearts not only close but sometimes *stay* closed. The major risk here is that we go through the motions of living without any sense of connection to the profound mystery that is always within us and around us.

On a less dramatic but nonetheless important level, as we grow older, we are particularly vulnerable to becoming bound by habit. Our eyes may be covered by "the veil of familiarity,"[3] and we might stop really *seeing* our beloved partner across the breakfast table, the mountains outside of our window, the golden retriever we walk in the park every morning, or our colleague of many years whose office is right across the hall from our own. We may find ourselves settling for mere images in our minds, a belief that we know what there is to know about life, and as the saying goes, "There is nothing new under the sun" (Eccles. 1:9).

My growing realization that mystery is fundamental to life took a giant leap forward when I decided to become a hospice volunteer in my late twenties. In the 1960s, the groundbreaking work of Elizabeth Kubler-Ross had helped to bring about a radical shift in our culture's view of death. She named and challenged the pervasive denial of death in the medical community and in society as a whole. By highlighting what a spiritually sensitive time it is when a person is approaching death, she inspired countless professionals and laypeople to realize what a gift it could be to serve the dying. In their books and retreats, spiritual teachers Ram Dass and Stephen Levine described the powerful transformations they experienced in working with people who were close to the end of their lives. Their inspiration was contagious. I felt a mixture of excitement and fear when I consciously decided to turn toward the reality of death instead of away from it, as I had been taught to do by my family and culture. As far back as my early twenties, I had an intuitive sense that death was the primary spiritual "teacher" in my life.

Rather than finding the topic morbid or depressing, I found it endlessly fascinating and completely enlivening. I began to understand a phrase I'd heard when I was in psychotherapy with a Gestalt therapist. He spoke of what he called our "growing edge." I could grasp the idea intellectually when I initially heard the phrase, and it soon started to make sense to me on an experiential level. This concept has played a central role in my inner guidance process for many years now. I've learned to appreciate the vulnerability and courage that are required to regularly visit the challenge zone it represents. Simply put, embracing the mystery requires a deep commitment to continuous emotional and spiritual growth, both for our own benefit and for the benefit of others. For me, keeping death in my awareness has served as an amazingly effective method for staying in touch with mystery and for inspiring me to awaken as quickly and fully as possible.

By the time I was thirty-three years old, I had become the first director of the Mesilla Valley Hospice, a new service organization in Las Cruces, New Mexico. Shortly after starting my position, I received a phone call from Michael, our medical director, and he asked me to visit an elderly couple at the local hospital. He told me their story, which, like many I was hearing in this new role, was a sad one. Jean and Harvey had recently moved to town from Boston, where they had lived and worked for forty-three years. Their two grown sons had moved out west, one to Denver and one to Phoenix. Harvey had sold his furniture business after slowly building it into a successful enterprise, and it was time to enjoy the fruits of their labors. At least, that was their plan.

Three weeks after moving into the apartment they rented, Harvey was diagnosed with lung cancer. He'd been through surgeries, radiation treatments, and several rounds of chemotherapy. His oncologist and his wife felt strongly that he could buy more time with another round of chemo. Jean, in her mid-seventies, was more or less living in Harvey's hospital room and was on the verge of becoming ill herself from the stress. Harvey had been a compliant patient up to this point, but for the first time he was questioning his doctor's judgment and the treatment process in general. My task was to meet with this couple and help them talk about whether Harvey would continue the chemotherapy treatments.

I knocked on the door of room 220 at St. Luke's Hospital. As I walked in, I noticed that even though the second bed in the room was empty, Jean and Harvey still had the privacy curtain closed around his bed. After introducing myself, I pulled up a chair next to Jean at Harvey's bedside. He was resting peacefully, eyes closed. She looked completely exhausted, as if she hadn't slept in days. She sat with rounded shoulders, half-reading a day-old newspaper. There was a smear of mustard on her cheek, probably left over from lunch. Overhearing my whispered conversation with Jean, Harvey roused and came to life. He had a pleasant smile and a welcoming look on his face. "Thanks so much for coming. Dr. Langley told us you'd be stopping by." We broke the ice with small talk, and I mostly listened, trying to understand what most needed to happen here.

After a few minutes, Jean turned to me and said, "I guess you're here to explain to Harvey why he should continue his treatments. The doctor said he could win a few more months, at least. And maybe more than that. He just has to keep fighting." I noticed Harvey's grimace when she used the word *fighting*. I had to suppress my own grimace when she used the word *win*. In my mind, what we were dealing with was neither a battle nor a game, yet I could see that she looked at the situation differently.

At that point, Harvey leaned forward and raised his bed so that he was more upright and better able to converse. He looked at Jean with deeply loving eyes, sighed audibly, and said in a soft voice, "Honey, I've had a really good, full life. When I feel this bad from side effects, a few extra months don't really help very much. I'm so tired, and I'm ready to go." Jean looked away for a moment and then began to weep. She'd known for a while that Harvey felt the way he did and that he'd been hanging on for her sake. I gently slid my chair back a bit from the bed and let these two people feel what was going on between them. "Besides," said Harvey, "if you don't go home and get some rest, you're going to be in the next bed one of these days." As the tears streamed down her cheeks, Jean realized it was time to loosen her grip. Time to give Harvey permission to leave the battlefield. Time for both of them to rest. She looked into his eyes and nodded slowly, a silent sign of surrender.

Harvey seemed both drained and relieved from the brief yet difficult conversation that had been so long coming. A palpable stillness hung in the room for a few minutes as they both withdrew into the privacy of their own hearts. Then Harvey lowered his bed and quickly fell into a deep sleep. I put my hand on Jean's shoulder, and we both quietly stood up and left the room.

As we walked down the hall, she told me she didn't want

to leave Harvey's side because she didn't want him to die alone. "Nobody should *ever* die alone," she said. I could see how important that was to her, and I could also see how exhausted she was from her long vigil at his bedside. "I'll tell you what," I said. "If you're willing to go home and take care of yourself for the night, I'll sleep in the empty bed in Harvey's room. That way, if he dies during the night, he won't be alone. And you'll get some of the rest you desperately need as well." She reluctantly agreed and then went back into the room to tell Harvey how much she loved him. Although he was sound asleep and she'd said the words countless times since he was diagnosed, she wanted to whisper them one more time. She seemed ready to release him.

When she came out, I said I'd walk her to her car, and we started down the hall. Quite suddenly, and with surprising intensity, she turned to me and in a hushed, in-the-hall-of-a-hospital voice, questioned me. "Why my Harvey? He's such a good man! There are all these evil people in the world. Why my Harvey?" From my phone call with our hospice medical director, I knew that Jean was a rational humanist who didn't like what she termed "childish God-talk." An image of Rabbi Levine came into my mind, and I modified the words I'd heard him speak those many years before. "Jean," I said, "there are some things that go on in the universe that we just don't understand."

The feeling that what happens in life is beyond our understanding is one that many of us experience at one time or another. So, too, is the feeling that life isn't fair or just. There's something about the utter finality of physical death, in particular, that is completely non-negotiable and often extremely difficult to accept.

Some of us are introduced to this incomprehensible or unfair aspect of reality when we're children. Perhaps a beloved grandparent dies or our pet is killed by a car. Perhaps our parents decide to divorce and the comforting safety of our family life disappears overnight. Perhaps we're diagnosed with an incurable chronic illness and we realize that we need to envision our future options in an entirely different way than before. Sometimes when we're given really terrible news we reflexively respond, "You're kidding!" as if someone we know well would joke about such suffering. A part of us understandably rebels, "This can't be. There must be some mistake. This was *not* in my plans."

I often see our struggle to understand an unexpected change to be a necessary avoidance of the raw emotions that are triggered when we experience loss, surprise, or tragedy. This kind of defense mechanism buys us time to expand our affect tolerance and to assimilate what has happened. When we wrestle with the *why* questions, we maintain a certain distance from the *what* questions like "What happened?" "What am I feeling?" and "What's going to happen to *me* now?" Because the answers we come up with to our *why* questions are often unsatisfying, we eventually realize that we're called upon to face this new reality as it actually is and to somehow learn to accept the fact that it is so.

An encounter with death is one of the most common

points of entry into the realm of mystery. Another doorway is the experience of childbirth. Regardless of how well we intellectually understand the biology of human reproduction, the experience of giving birth or of witnessing a birth introduces many of us to the sheer power of the life force and the true awesomeness of our existence. For me, death and birth merged completely one summer night in New Mexico.

It started out as an ordinary workday at the hospice in Las Cruces, where I'd then been working for nine months. I was beginning to feel like I knew my way around town and had a handle on the transition I'd recently made from executive director to clinical director. We had a team meeting in the early morning, and I then headed over to the hospital to see a potential new patient.

The discharge planner had spoken to Maria at some length about our hospice program, and Maria seemed to agree that hospice care was an appropriate next step. Still, she wanted to meet one of our staff people, and I was happy to put a human face on our organization as well as to answer her questions. As it turned out, she didn't have any real questions she couldn't answer for herself. What she really wanted was to share her story and to prepare for the end of what she called "my life in this world."

This was the kind of listening experience I had come to savor, one in which I could be wholeheartedly present with a deep appreciation for the exquisite uniqueness of each moment and each person's life. Maria spoke about growing up in Mexico and living with her aunt and uncle for several years after her parents moved to the United States.

Her accent was still quite pronounced, though I could follow almost everything she said. She became teary when she described being a young child and hearing her two older brothers talk about whether they would ever see their parents again. A devout Catholic, she said she had always trusted that "God would reunite our family when He thought the time was right." She was eleven when her parents contacted her aunt and said it was time to send the children.

Her story unfolded from there, and in the fifty-five minutes I sat with her, I came to appreciate what a rich and challenging life this woman had experienced. Now in her early eighties, with cancer spreading throughout much of her body, she knew she was likely to die soon. I had the sense that she knew in her heart that she probably had just days left to live. Other than introducing myself and exchanging a few pleasantries when I first entered the room, I had hardly spoken a word to Maria. I had given her my full attention, listening intently to what she had to say and making it clear to her that I was willing to bear witness as she made peace with the life she had lived.

When it was time for me to leave, I thanked her for telling me about her life and explained that I would be one of the hospice people who would visit her at home when she left the hospital in a couple days. I walked toward the door to her room and turned to take one more look at her. She had leaned back on the elevated hospital bed, closed her eyes, and seemed to be resting comfortably. I still remember wondering if I would ever see her alive again.

That night, I joined some friends for dinner at their

home. My friend Tim was a physical therapist who worked in a group practice in town. His very pregnant wife, Monica, was a dancer and yoga practitioner who was due any day. Our close mutual friend, Eddie, was a massage therapist who shared an office suite with Tim.

We filled up on tortilla chips, homemade salsa, delicious vegetarian burritos, and good conversation. Our conversation flowed comfortably, with laughter bubbling up often. The main topic was how we each felt about living in Las Cruces. All of us were transplants from different parts of the United States, and we each had a unique mix of feelings about living in southern New Mexico.

About a half hour into the meal, Monica excused herself and went to the bathroom. It was a little before 9:00 P.M. "Tim," she called out, after she'd been gone a couple of minutes. "Come here, please. I don't think this is pee." Tim popped up from his place at the table and walked through the living room to the bathroom. "Really? Are you sure?" Eddie and I heard him say. When he reentered the dining room, he looked white and pasty. "Monica's water broke, and our baby is on the way. . . . I'm supposed to call the midwife." Eddie and I got up and walked him over to the phone in the kitchen. "OK, now call the midwife," Eddie said in a calm, firm voice. After a brief exchange, Tim hung up. "She'll be here in thirty to forty minutes."

Tim stood there looking shell-shocked and didn't move. "I'd suggest you go check on Monica," I said. When he left the room, Eddie and I discussed what we should do. "Let's wait until the midwife gets here and then quietly slip out," he said. That seemed reasonable to me. Our plan changed abruptly when Tim came back to the dining room table. "Monica and I just talked, and we'd like it if you guys would stay and help us with the birth." That possibility had never entered my mind and apparently hadn't entered Eddie's either, but how could we say anything but yes to such a trusting and special request? "Sure," we said simultaneously.

What words can do justice to seeing a baby enter this world? Monica and the midwife, Danielle, were an amazing team. Tim and Eddie massaged Monica and helped her deal with her back pain when it became really intense. I did some guided relaxation with her and helped Tim stay grounded and present when he started to overreact at times. The whole process went smoothly and according to their birthing plan. This was a first experience for all of us (except the midwife, of course). Danielle seemed to be totally in her element, expressing a perfect balance of heart and mind, intuition and intellect.

It was 2:10 A.M. when Eddie and I walked out of the house. The July night air was still and welcoming. Looking up at a cloudless sky, I could see that the moon was full. Eddie and I exchanged a hug, muttered a few adjectives, and shook our heads in mutual amazement. He got into his car and left. I looked up at the brilliant moon and came to a new, improved understanding of what the word *wonder* actually means. In the morning, I had visited someone who was preparing to leave this world. In the evening, I had helped someone brand-new to enter this world. What did it all mean? *Perhaps I'll never really know*, I thought to myself. *And that's just fine with me.*

What I felt at that moment brings to mind a phrase I first heard when a mentor and friend, Father Thomas Keating, spoke at a 1983 conference at Naropa University. It was a Buddhist-Christian dialogue conference, and whenever Father Thomas wanted to talk about God—a word infrequently used in Buddhist circles—he substituted the phrase "the ultimate mystery." Everyone in the room—Christians, Jews, Buddhists, Hindus, Muslims, Wiccans, Sikhs, humanists, atheists, and unaffiliated people—seemed to feel at home with that phrase. It was as if we all knew, on a deep primordial level, that life and death are fundamentally a mystery to be lived and celebrated rather than a problem to be solved. This is one of the open secrets of the world's great wisdom traditions. By turning *toward* the unknowable mystery at the center of existence, we can learn to live and love well, to age with grace, and to die peacefully.

FINDING MYSTERY IN THE ORDINARY

Though they make for such excellent gateways to mystery, birth and death are quite infrequent events for most of us. But we need not wait for such singularly powerful experiences to embrace the mystery of our lives. Embracing mystery—the first of the seven keys to waking up in this life—is made easily accessible by the fact that the most ordinary of our experiences can also become a gateway to the ineffable. Thich Nhat Hanh understands the amazing potential inherent in routine daily life activities. His phrase "the miracle of mindfulness" tells the story. Thay, as his students and friends call him, recognizes the power of simple presence and the way it actualizes our innate capacity to see the sacred in the ordinary.

One of the skillful practices he has taught over the years is using a *gatha*, a short mindfulness recitation, to sacralize a daily action that has become unconscious and automatic. We have a deeply conditioned tendency to live as if we're on autopilot, sleepwalking through our day with no recognition of how precious it is to be alive in the first place. Imagine approaching a sink full of dinner dishes, stopping to take a deep, mindful breath, and then slowly reciting these words:

Washing the dishes
is like bathing a baby Buddha.
The profane is the sacred.
Everyday mind is Buddha's mind.[4]

Implicit in Thay's teaching is a reminder that we can explore the edge of mystery without waiting to be called to the bedside of a dying person or asked to help out at a home birth. We don't have to go on a six-month silent retreat or ingest a mind-altering substance. We simply have to step out of the self-created fantasy that so often separates us from ourselves, others, and the world. This stepping out happens organically and unexpectedly at times, in a way that some people associate with grace. At other times, we're required to practice "joyful exertion" to cut through the dense fog of delusion that distorts our perception of what's true. The good news is that we can learn to relinquish our obsession with the information, mastery, and control we imagine will assuage our existential anxiety. Opening to things as they are on a moment-to-moment basis, we gradually learn to trust our unfolding lives and to relax into the not-knowing that is ever present and ultimately unavoidable.

The writer Wendell Berry captured this view of awakening in an essay about what he called *our real work*:

> It may be that when we no longer know what to do
> we have come to our real work,
> and that when we no longer know which way to go
> we have come to our real journey.
> The mind that is not baffled is not employed.
> The impeded stream is the one that sings.[5]

Another time-tested approach to familiarizing ourselves with the mystery of our existence is to contemplate a perennial question that plays a central role in numerous wisdom traditions: "Who am I?" At first glance the answer seems so obvious that the question itself appears to be absurd. Perhaps that's why it became the subject of a story about the traditional Sufi "wise-fool," Mullah Nasruddin.

The story goes that Nasruddin walked into a bank one day in ancient Persia. He looked rather scruffy and unkempt, so the teller eyed him suspiciously when Nasruddin asked to cash a large check. The teller took the check, looked at a list of bad checks that were known to be circulating in town, and saw that the check appeared to be legitimate. Still feeling uneasy, he gazed at Nasruddin and said, "Well, this check appears to be fine. But can you identify yourself?" Nasruddin thought about the question for a few moments. Then he pulled a small hand mirror from his jacket pocket, looked into it, and smiled. "Yep. That's me all right," he replied.

A lot of us have a similar attitude to Nasruddin's. We've spent most of our lives with a recognizable sense of identity, one that appears to be consistent and stable over time. Like Nasruddin, we *think* we know who we are. We have a body and a personality that have become quite familiar and predictable. We know our home address, our phone number, our social security number, and our work résumé. As we move through childhood and adolescence and into adulthood, our self-talk and the responses of other people regularly reinforce this sense of a separate self—a self that, in reality, only represents one aspect of who we are. Inevitably, our confidence that we fully know ourselves is challenged by life, and we begin to see through the apparent solidity of the small self.

Those of us in midlife and elderhood are especially susceptible to this kind of disillusionment. When we work in the same job for two, three, or four decades, it's easy to see how and why we identify with our role at work. We don't say to people who ask about our job, "I work as a landscape architect." We say, "I *am* a landscape architect." In other words, my job defines "who I am" more than simply "what

I do." And because we live in an achievement-oriented society in which certain jobs have higher pay scales and more prestige associated with them, our self-esteem is often directly tied to where we are in a vocational pecking order, with chutes and ladders that go up and down. In view of causes and conditions like those just mentioned, it's easy to see how we form fixed beliefs about who we are and who other people are as well.

I've observed a similar process in the realm of intimate partnerships. I've been with my wife, Marsha, for more than thirty years. I've come to think of the phrase "Marsha and David" as one term that I use in a similar manner to how I use my own name. This makes sense in that our relationship is its own entity and exists in a way that is distinguishable from "David" or "Marsha" alone. While this is not a problem, per se, it can easily become one when there's a major change in our situation. I've sat with many people over the years who have lost a longtime partner to death or a breakup. Frequently, these people express how they feel with words like these: "I don't know who I am without Charlene in my life. We've been so intertwined for so long I feel like I'm starting over or starting anew. I often feel lost, confused, disoriented." This relates to the second meaning of *Life, Part Two* to which I referred earlier.

What usually happens in these situations is that we enter an in-between zone, a psychological mindscape that the writer William Bridges calls "the neutral zone."[6] Tibetan Buddhists refer to this inner terrain as the *bardo*. We know we're not who we used to be, and we don't yet know who we're becoming. Because this is a time of great fluidity in terms of who we think we are, it's an excellent opportunity to directly experience the process-nature of the true self that gives rise to our ego identity.

From a spiritual perspective, a central task in the second half of life is to recognize our dual nature, fully befriending our ego-self while at the same time realizing our ultimate identity, which has been given different names in different traditions. Whether we call it Buddha nature, Christ Consciousness, Interbeing, Big Mind, or True Self, words fall short and will never adequately capture the ineffable vastness, mystery, and love of who and what we really are on the deepest level. This education in how to live on two planes of consciousness at the same time is more likely to occur during the second half of life, and yet it is certainly not limited to older people in long-standing jobs or relationships. Sometimes a traumatic incident is the trigger, regardless of a person's age.

When I was working as a psychotherapist in the early 1990s, a twenty-six-year-old man who was finishing a Ph.D. in psychology began coming to see me. Derek was halfway through his doctoral dissertation and had already been encouraged to publish it as a book. His intellect had served him very well throughout his life, and he was looking forward to a long, productive career as a college professor. Then he lost control of his car one day and hit a tree. On one hand, he was quite fortunate because he escaped with just a few scratches and abrasions rather than broken bones or worse. On the other hand, he had a serious closed head injury that left him with pronounced cognitive deficits.

In a matter of moments, Derek went from being someone whose intellectual gifts were his defining characteristic to someone who was unable to read or write. His word-finding capacity was greatly diminished, as was his ability to process and retain information. His speech became slow, and he spoke haltingly, with long pauses. A neuropsychologist assessed his head injury and set him up with a regular program of computer exercises to help with his recovery process. When she told him it would take up to two years before she knew how much he would heal from the symptoms he was experiencing, he became noticeably disheartened and distressed. That's when she suggested that he also work with me.

Derek was somewhat withdrawn and guarded in our first meeting, but he gradually opened up during the three years we worked together. Initially, I helped him to grieve, to accept that his carefully crafted life plan had gone awry. He took a leave of absence from his doctoral program and applied himself to his cognitive exercises and psychotherapy sessions with admirable determination. Derek later described the most challenging aspect of his new life by saying, "I don't feel like myself anymore. I used to know who I was and where I was going. Now I feel lost at sea, adrift in a small rowboat on a dark, foggy night."

I'm delighted to say that this particular story has a happy ending. Derek did gradually heal from his brain injury. While it took him two years longer than planned to finish his Ph.D. program, he recovered almost all of his former intellectual abilities and went on to develop a highly successful private practice. It may come as no surprise that he chose to make the neuropsychology of trauma resolution his practice specialty and became a respected trainer in that field.

Many of us have had or will have some kind of experience in which our very identity is called into question. We might become a parent or grandparent for the first time and develop a radically new vision of what's important in life. We might lose a job and return to school to retrain in a new field. We might have a serious health crisis and have to give up our favorite activities. We might fall deeply in love with a future mate just as we're planning to enter a three-year meditation retreat (this one has personal significance). We might be given a large inheritance or be forced to sell a farm that has been in our family for generations.

Although we're skilled at convincing ourselves otherwise, much of the time we have a very limited amount of control over the external events in our lives. It's also true that the events that make the limits of our control clear can teach us that there is much more to who and what we are than most of us have ever imagined. Indeed, wise spiritual teachers often advise us to view our life experiences as a curriculum for awakening to our true nature. This is the sacred task in any consciously lived life. Whether or not we reach the theoretical endpoint of the journey is not the issue. What matters is the aspiration, the purity of heart that inspires us to continually open into the great unknown and become living instruments of its inherent goodness.

Ram Dass, a much-loved spiritual teacher who played a major role in waking up the baby boom generation and continued to be a beacon of elder wisdom until his death in December 2019, described the process of embracing "the ultimate mystery" in his classic book, *Be Here Now*:

> What is happening to you is nothing less than death and rebirth. What is dying is the entire way in which you understood "who you are" and "how it all is." What is being reborn is the child of the Spirit for whom things all are new. This process of attending an ego that is dying at the same time as you are going through a birth process is awesome. Be gentle and honor him (self) that is dying as well as him (Self) who is being born.[7]

CHAPTER TWO
CHOOSING A VISION

This is how a human being can change:
There's a worm addicted to eating grape leaves.
Suddenly, he wakes up, call it Grace, whatever,
something wakes him, and he's no longer a worm.

He's the entire vineyard, and the orchard, too,
the fruit, the trunks, a growing wisdom and joy
that doesn't need to devour.

—RUMI

RETURNING AGAIN and again to a sense of ultimate mystery involves a significant amount of practice. There are exceptions—moments of grace or profound communion—in which the numinous aspect of life and death seems to come to us or to come from within us. But for most of us most of the time, maintaining an ongoing awareness of mystery requires a long-term commitment. This is generally not something that comes easily. It requires openness, effort, and attention, not to mention humility and a willingness to learn and adjust. We are unlikely to sustain these qualities without a clear sense of direction and a strong sense of purpose. This brings us immediately into contact with another key aspect of aging gracefully in the second half of life. We sincerely ask the question "Toward what end?" in relation to the time we have on this earth. Said another way, what is our vision for the life we are living at this stage in our journey?

Some of us may recoil from this question, seeing it as an unhelpful cul-de-sac of metaphysical speculation and striving after pipe dreams. If that's your experience, try rephrasing the question in a language that resonates for you. You might prefer to ask, "What matters to me most, and to what extent is that a part of my life right now?" Or you might reflect on which upcoming activities cause you to start a new day with feelings of excitement and aliveness. One person I worked with used the following question as a regular check-in with herself: "Am I living the life I most deeply want to be living?" She would sometimes follow up the first question with a second that she learned from her study of the great Jewish teacher Rabbi Hillel: "If not now, when?"

For me, the original version of the question—"What is my vision for the life I'm living at this stage in my journey?"—works well. I find that this particular inquiry triggers a deep inward listening that plays a central role in the choices I make. I believe the way we choose to live our lives is heavily influenced by an underlying vision, whether we're aware of what that vision is or not.

When we're out of touch with our hearts' deepest desires, we stumble haphazardly from one experience to another in search of some kind of lasting satisfaction. When we're in clear contact with our vision for living, we tap into the remarkable power of *intention*, and we take the necessary steps to bring our lives into alignment with our core values. There's a quiet yet robust feeling of well-being that arises in our hearts as we increasingly live the lives we most deeply want to live. Although our vision is never set in stone and may change, sometimes in surprising ways, it continually functions like the North Star guiding a ship at sea. It enables us to make decisions in present time that will shape the way our future unfolds. We sense the possibility of living with true integrity, and that inspires us to continue on the path of spiritual realization in a wholehearted way.

In emphasizing the value of a clear vision that guides us through our lives, I'm not suggesting that it's easy to identify and articulate a guiding light of this kind. Some of us were passionate young adults who felt focused and energized by our ideals and sense of limitless possibilities. Others of us wandered through our teen and young adult years like lost souls without a compass or a map. In both cases, a lot of us watched our ideals fall by the wayside as the practical realities of life gradually deflated our enthusiasm and hopefulness. Many of us have felt a need to adjust our personal vision to create a shared vision with an intimate partner or family. We may be raising one or more children, caring for aging parents, *and* working full-time jobs.

It's common to feel that there's not much time or energy for contemplative engagement with an imaginary future.

Looking back at my own life, I can see how the painful confusion and alienation I felt as a young person was related to a lack of vision in my life. This was particularly true after my father died and I started asking questions that were more characteristic of a person in midlife than a thirteen-year-old. The materialistic values of the middle-class suburb in which I was raised made no sense to me whatsoever. Everyone around me seemed to care deeply about things that meant little or nothing to me—how much money this person earned, what kind of car that person drove, who won this week's Cleveland Browns football game, what label was on a pair of jeans, who got into Harvard, and who was going to the local community college. With death on my shoulder, why would I possibly care about any of that seeming nonsense?

Much of the time, I felt more than a little crazy. While I knew what didn't matter to me, I had no idea what *did*. So, I often went along with the crowd and acted as if I cared about the same things everyone else seemed to care about. This charade continued through my first year and a half of college. The late 1960s, with its counterculture, race riots, assassinations, protests, and Vietnam War, was an intense time to come of age. Partying, promiscuity, drugs, alcohol—these were more or less the norm at Tulane University.

What better city is there than New Orleans in which to sow wild oats?

Without knowing it, I was doing personal research on the Buddhist notion of *samsara*, the wheel of suffering that we experience when we're lost in a seemingly endless cycle of craving, aversion, and delusion. There seemed to be no light at the end of the tunnel and no motivation to continue the status quo. I gradually slipped into a painful blend of depression and anxiety. It was easily recognizable from the abnormal psychology course I was taking as part of my degree program. That's when I got my first glimpse of what the word *grace* is all about. On my twenty-first birthday, I noticed a book on a friend's bookshelf and asked to borrow it. "Sure," he said, "just bring it back when you're done."

It was a book on yoga, both the physical postures and the spiritual philosophy associated with them. Finding it hard to put down, I read it the way people read a best-selling mystery thriller. Using the diagrams in the book, I started teaching myself hatha yoga postures. The book also introduced the practice of meditation, which gave me my first glimpse of a way to work effectively with difficult moods and emotions. With the zeal of a religious convert, I began to see that there was an alternative to the nihilistic worldview I had been unconsciously turning into a self-fulfilling prophecy.

I practiced and studied enthusiastically for about six months on my own, at which point I realized I needed a qualified teacher to continue to progress. Attending a ten-day retreat program with Swami Satchidananda, a respected teacher who had moved from India to New York to teach in the West, made it clear to me that he was just such a teacher. As I deepened my meditation practice and more fully embraced the lifestyle that Satchidananda taught, I began to notice the return of an inner peace and a lightness of being that had left me when I entered kindergarten. I experienced moments of "happiness for no reason," as Tibetan Buddhist teacher Matthieu Ricard puts it.[1] Without really knowing what I was doing, I had discovered a way of living that was rooted in an ancient and timeless vision. Swami Satchidananda described this perspective in his book *Integral Yoga Hatha*:

> A body of perfect health and strength, mind with all clarity and calmness, intellect as sharp as a razor, will as pliable as steel, life full of dedication, and Realization of the True Self is the goal of Integral Yoga. Attain this through asanas, pranayama, chanting of Holy Names, self-discipline, selfless action, mantra japa, meditation, study, and reflection.[2]

At first glance, a vision of this kind sounds like an incredibly tall order. If we're not cautious, it can easily feed into our tendency toward ego inflation or the self-criticism of our frequently harsh superegos. On the other hand, when wisely understood and skillfully utilized, this kind of vision can get us out of bed each morning with a spring in our step and excitement about the day. We may begin to see our lives as purposeful, part of a transformational process that thoughtful human beings have found to be completely trustworthy for millennia.

THE ROLE OF ASPIRATION IN CREATING A VISION

What's important when exploring our vision is that we understand the difference between *aspirations* and *expectations* in the realm of spiritual training. Expectations, particularly of ourselves, are often unrealistically high. Like a reverberating echo deep in our psyches, there is often a voice that says with a tone of sadness, anger, or despair, *Not good enough. Still not lovable. Something's wrong with you. You are so broken.* This "mood of unlove," as transpersonal psychologist John Welwood dubbed it, is sometimes so deep-seated in the unconscious that we stopped noticing it long ago.[3] Instead, our bodies and emotional habits tell the story—we walk and sit with rounded shoulders, looking beaten down from years of self-judgment. Our flattened affect offers further evidence of how defeated we feel. Now we're adding a new, long list of behaviors and character traits that we'll never be able to live up to. Another vision statement captures our predicament in down-to-earth language:

> If you can start the day without caffeine or pep pills,
> If you can be cheerful, ignoring aches and pains,
> If you can resist complaining and boring people with
> your troubles,

If you can eat the same food every day and be grateful
    for it,
If you can understand when loved ones are too busy
    to give you time,
If you can overlook when people take things out on
    you when, through no fault of yours, something
    goes wrong,
If you can take criticism and blame without
    resentment,
If you can face the world without lies and deceit,
If you can conquer tension without medical help,
If you can relax without liquor,
If you can sleep without the aid of drugs,
Then you are probably a dog or a cat.

Needless to say, it's better to have no vision at all than to reinforce our low self-esteem by comparing ourselves to an imaginary being who embodies absolute perfection. The wounded child inside so many of us lives in a world of scarcity in which there is a limited amount of love and validation to go around. Comparing ourselves to a super-lofty ideal is guaranteed to create suffering as we rub against the fact that we don't measure up and know we never will.

On the other hand, when we understand the role of aspiration and its function in spiritual development, we aim our hearts in the direction of our highest vision and recognize that its purpose is to give us a sense of direction. Just as the ship on the ocean never physically touches the North Star, we will not reach the theoretical endpoint of our transformational journey. Our vision guides us onward, however, and inspires us to continue our inner and outer training as impeccably as we're able. When we're involved in a church, a sangha, a mosque, a *satsang*, a synagogue, or any authentic community of like-minded aspirants, this effect is amplified by the commonality of vision. Like geese flying in formation, we support one another as we each cultivate our best human qualities.

What are some other examples of skillful and constructive visions from which people draw strength and encouragement? Here's one from the first Psalm of the Hebrew scriptures:

> Blessed are the man and the woman
> > who have grown beyond their greed
> > and have put an end to their hatred
> > and no longer nourish illusions.
> But they delight in the way things are
> > and keep their hearts open, day and night.
> They are like trees planted near flowing rivers,
> > which bear fruit when they are ready.
> Their leaves will not fall or wither.
> > Everything they do will succeed.[4]

We see a delightful example of these very qualities in a conversation that Mother Teresa of Calcutta once had with an interviewer from *Time* magazine. He expressed his admiration for her many works of service and charity. "How do you do it, Mother?" he asked. "I don't claim anything of the work," she said. "I'm just a little pencil in God's hand."[5]

In one simple sentence, Mother Teresa expressed the energizing vision that gave direction to her extraordinary life and the lives of the women in her order, the Missionaries of Charity. Having closely followed and studied her life and work, I don't believe she was speaking with false humility. Rather, she had given herself over so completely to the Divine that she only wished to be used by her Beloved as an instrument of service for those in need. She referred to these people as "the poorest of the poor" and "Christ in his distressing disguise." A quotation often attributed to her summarizes her approach to living: "Not all of us can do great things. But we can do small things with great love."

The Dalai Lama is another well-loved spiritual teacher whose life inspires people all over the world, regardless of their religious affiliation or lack thereof. Among other things, he's known for teachings that go right to the heart of true religiosity at its best. Once he was asked about Tibetan Buddhism by a reporter, who probably anticipated a long, complex response. Instead, the Dalai Lama said simply, "My religion is kindness." For decades, he has tirelessly traveled the world, reminding us that when it comes to the things that matter most, we have a lot more in common than we realize. "We all want to be happy," he frequently says. "None of us wants to suffer." He speaks of the need for each of us to accept "universal responsibility" for the world we create together and the importance of each of us cultivating "a good heart." In comments and teachings like these, the Dalai Lama reveals his vision for his own life, which is to be what he calls "a force for good." He invites each of us to do the same, in whatever way is appropriate for us.

In the Mahayana tradition of Buddhism, we find a fascinating and challenging vision that plays an integral role in the life of the practitioner. Millions of Buddhists around the world regularly recite or chant the "bodhisattva vow" as part of their daily practice. Interestingly, their vow combines the two elements of spiritual awakening that we've been exploring in this book—mystery and vision. The central aspiration in the Mahayana tradition is to become a bodhisattva, one who commits their life to becoming fully enlightened so they can liberate all living beings from suffering. At first glance, the aspiration involved seems so impossible as to be foolish. While there are diverse expressions of this commitment, they all emphasize the same basic intentions. Here's one traditional version of the bodhisattva vow:

> Suffering beings are numberless; I vow to liberate them all.
> Attachment is inexhaustible; I vow to release it all.
> The gates to truth are numberless; I vow to master them all.
> The ways of awakening are supreme; I vow to realize them all.[6]

Wherein lies the mystery? In the obvious impossibility of accomplishing the goals that are mentioned in these vows. What's the point of setting ourselves up for failure? It's completely clear that no human being could accomplish what the bodhisattva hopes to achieve. What we see here is an emphasis on intention that plays a very important role in Buddhist teachings, especially the teachings on karma.

The Buddha taught that it's the intention behind our actions that determines the effect of those actions on our character and our future. As mentioned previously, we often have little or no control over certain events in our lives. Still, we can choose to cultivate wholesome motivation. It's this understanding that inspires spiritual practitioners who envision themselves as "bodhisattvas in training." They come to see what's possible when purity of heart combines with skillful action to benefit those in need. In sustaining this kind of life-defining vision over an extended period of time, practitioners realize that the essence of the bodhisattva's way of life is to become an increasingly effective instrument of healing while gradually learning to relinquish attachment to the fruits of their actions. It's as if they die into their activities and become living statements of selfless service.

A related Zen teaching offers an additional perspective that I've found to be both grounding and uplifting. In that our minds have a strong tendency to fall into either-or thinking, it's important to remind ourselves on a regular basis that whatever reality is, it's much more accurately understood as "both-and" or, in some cases, "all of the

above." Choosing an integrative vision like the one that follows is a very helpful way to avoid being trapped in a small,
contracted sense of self that struggles with one inner conflict after another.

> The Master in the art of living
> makes little distinction between his work and his play,
> his labor and his leisure,
> his mind and his body,
> his education and his recreation,
> his love and his religion.
> He hardly knows which is which.
> He simply pursues his vision
> of excellence in whatever he does,
> leaving others to decide whether he is working
> or playing. To him he is always doing both.[7]

One of the most transformative visions for my life was
literally a vision I experienced at St. Benedict's Monastery
in Old Snowmass, Colorado, in the spring of 1981. On the
suggestion of a friend, I had sought out Father Thomas
Keating, the recently arrived guest master at the monastery.
The drive from Boulder to Old Snowmass was a beautiful
meditation of a sort. Driving through the splendor of the
Roaring Fork Valley, my eyes were constantly pulled toward
the majestic beauty of Mount Sopris, which, at thirteen
thousand feet, seemed to watch over the entire area like a
vigilant sentinel.

After settling into my room in the small gatehouse the monks used for overnight guests, I walked the hundred yards or so to the monastery bookstore. Father Thomas met me there as planned, and we spoke of our mutual friend, Father Theophane Boyd, whom I had met at a meditation retreat in Massachusetts the previous fall. Since I had reached St. Benedict's in the early afternoon, he asked if I'd had any lunch, and when I said no, he walked me over to the kitchen, pointed out the leftovers, and said, "Please help yourself." As I ate, we talked about my interest in Aldous Huxley's book *The Perennial Philosophy* and my desire to learn about the Centering Prayer. Father Thomas and some other monks had recently adapted an ancient prayer practice from a mystical fourteenth-century text called *The Cloud of Unknowing*, and they were teaching it to an increasing number of people who were requesting, "Teach me to pray."

This wise and gentle teacher listened with rapt attention and spoke in a thoughtful, measured way. He looked relaxed and completely present. The calmness of his being filled and enfolded me in a way that felt strangely unfamiliar. "Well," he said, when there was a pause in the conversation, "let me tell you about the Centering Prayer." He explained the history of the prayer, including its ancient roots and the way he and another monk had "repackaged" the prayer to make it accessible to modern spiritual seekers. The instructions he gave me were simple, clear, and direct. I noted the similarities to Eastern meditation practices I had done; however, this method had more of the devotional flavor I was seeking at that time. "If you'd like,

I'll stop by tomorrow morning after Lauds [the morning service that begins shortly after sunrise] and see if you have any questions," he offered. "That would be great," I replied. "Thank you so much for your time today." He smiled, held my gaze a moment, nodded, and left.

The stillness of the gatehouse and the silence of the monastery enchanted me for the rest of the evening. I had forgotten the extent to which ambient noise like traffic sounds and leaf blowers registered in my nervous system until they were completely absent. I made a simple dinner of soup, salad, and bread; read part of a Thomas Merton book on contemplative prayer that was on the gatehouse bookshelf; and went to bed. I slept deeply and woke up early, eager to try the new practice I had been taught.

I started with the Lord's Prayer, repeating it one line at a time and allowing a pause for reflection before going on to the next line. Working with a God-centered practice after six years of Buddhist training felt odd at first, as if I were visiting a foreign country. At the same time, my heart felt so happy to have an outlet for all the unexpressed love it contained. I understood what Father Thomas had said about the use of a "prayer word" and the way in which it was different from a mantra in Eastern teachings. He had suggested using it in the manner that a raptor uses its wings when riding the thermals. It lets go and soars with the wind much of the time, and only now and then, when it wants to change altitude or direction, it flaps its wings once or twice to direct its movement through space. The felt sense of the practice was tender and restful, like fully relaxing in the arms of a loved one who knew me better than I knew myself.

As I continued the Centering Prayer practice, I remembered a dream I'd had during the night. Most of the content was out of reach, and yet I recalled the ending with crystal clarity. I had been presented with a choice and felt compelled to make a decision: would I be the son of my own natural mother or the son of Mother Mary? I had woken up still wrestling with what to do. As I sat in the early morning stillness thinking of that dream and practicing the Centering Prayer, I experienced a vision completely out of the blue. It had a numinous quality, a luminescence that was shimmering with vivid aliveness. It was an image of Mother Mary holding the baby Jesus in her arms. She was radiant and larger than life, and I was looking up at her in the way I had looked up at the stained-glass image of her in the front of the monastery church.

Tears began to stream down my cheeks. I felt deeply loved and lovable in a way that I had never known was possible. The intensely painful wound in my heart that led me to feel so broken, so ashamed, so unfixable, so hopeless, was finally being seen and acknowledged. Even as this was happening, I recognized the fact that Mother Mary was as much a part of me as she was something outside myself. The same was true of the baby Jesus in her arms. I also understood that, on the most profound level, the love I was feeling was not an "object" that could be given and received. It was actually my own true nature and the nature of ultimate reality itself. This loving awareness, symbolized by Mary and Jesus, was what I had been searching for my whole life. The cosmic humor in the situation, that I was a Jewish Buddhist learning to pray at a Catholic monastery and having a vision of Mother Mary and the baby Jesus, did not escape me. Somehow, that made the whole experience even more joyful and amazing.

Eventually, I gathered myself together, washed my face, and had some breakfast. Father Thomas would be coming by soon, and I knew he would want to talk about my morning prayer. I wondered if I would be able to find words that would even come close to capturing what had happened.

Father Thomas knocked on the door and I invited him in. After sitting down across from me, he asked how it had gone with the Centering Prayer this morning. I described my experience, reliving it somewhat as I spoke. As I sat with him, I recognized the same profound feeling of lovingkindness I had experienced in the vision. I was so self-involved when telling the story that I hadn't noticed what was going on with Father Thomas. When I finished, I looked at him and saw that he had tears in his eyes. "What grace," he said in a hushed voice like the one people use in an ancient European cathedral. "What grace." We looked at each other for a long time, words feeling completely unnecessary. He got up to leave, and I walked him to the gatehouse door. We shared a warm hug, and he headed back to the monastery.

This experience confirmed, in my innermost reality, my intuition that unconditional love need not be just a lofty concept or an ever-receding spiritual horizon that is a source of sadness, yearning, and frustration. It can be an actuality in a human life. I realized on a cellular level that the love that had temporarily filled me, surrounded me, and completely transformed my being was not something to be collected. It was not a commodity to be bartered, a moral imperative, or an action to be performed. Rather, the loving awareness that gave rise to the vision was *who I was and am now* on the deepest level—just as it is who we all are, have always been, and will always be. My task in life, as I've come to understand it, is to remember who I really am and to help others do the same in as skillful and compassionate a way as I'm able. That's how this literal vision gave birth to a new road map for living the rest of my life, blessing me with a new vision and a passionate sense of purpose. I was thirty-one years old when I met Father Thomas. The last forty years have been significantly shaped by what happened that spring morning in the monastery guesthouse at St. Benedict's.

A central guideline for choosing a vision becomes clear when we reflect on the examples offered in this chapter. There are many different ways to identify and express our aspirations to live an awakened life. There's no "right" way to complete this task. We embody different racial backgrounds, ethnicities, abilities and disabilities, socioeconomic groups, religious viewpoints, gender identities, and sexual orientations. We have our own histories, strengths, weaknesses, commitments, and preferences. It makes sense, then, that we each articulate and manifest our highest vision in a unique manner.

For your vision to energize your unfolding on the spiritual path, it must be truly your own, something that aligns with your most cherished values. That's not to say you shouldn't incorporate the values, priorities, and ways of living you learn from the wisdom teachings of a particular religion or from the perennial philosophy. It does mean you have to do a certain kind of inner work in order to embrace your vision with integrity, even if that vision initially was expressed by someone else.

One way to do this inner work is to study the intentions and goals of spiritual guides you respect. This kind of exploration enables you to try out various "maps" that provide a sense of orientation on the spiritual path. You notice the similarities and differences between teachers, and the differences in particular give you permission to find your own way in the visioning process. I find it important to remember that a vision functions for a certain period of time as what Buddhists call a "skillful means"; it's not something to cling to as if it were permanent. We can be playful and creative as we explore the choice points and possibilities, staying in touch with the joy of simple presence as we participate in the ongoing adventure that is life. A vision of conscious living, when wisely understood, informs how we live on a moment-to-moment basis without creating what in the Zen tradition is called "a gaining attitude."

In my own practice, I find it helpful to periodically express my vision in writing. Doing so requires that I clarify and organize my thoughts, feelings, values, and insights. Because I've been writing about my understanding of awakening for many years, I've observed how my ideas continue to evolve over time. This has given birth to a recognition that words can only go so far in expressing our true nature, and they are best understood as the proverbial fingers pointing toward the moon of direct personal experience. The following is an example of a personal vision I wrote about seven years ago when I was reflecting on my original aspiration to live an awakened life.

A MORNING PRAYER

Thank you for this new day now beginning.
Thank you for the passage through the night.
Thank you for the gifts and blessings,
challenges and teachings,
miracles and mysteries
of this most amazing life.

Grant your blessings, my teachers and guides,
that in all that I say and think and do this day,
I may be an instrument of the precious Dharma,
an instrument of healing, blessing, and liberation.
Let my life be an expression of love and wisdom,
peace and joy, truth and freedom,
that I and all beings, without exception of any kind,
may awaken together and live in harmony
with the Great Way that is beyond all names and
        forms.

That is my heartfelt prayer.

May it be so.

I start most of my days by reciting this prayer before I get out of bed. If my wife, Marsha, is still asleep when I decide to get up, I recite it to myself subvocally. If she's gotten out of bed before me and I'm alone, I generally recite the prayer aloud in a soft voice, as if I'm in conversation with my spiritual teachers as well as with the ultimate mystery that is their source. Admittedly, there are days when it feels like a rote exercise, something a child might speed through in church or synagogue every weekend. Most days, however, it functions like a celebratory splash of cold water in my face. It's a reminder of what matters most to me, a recognition of the importance of gratitude for the gifts of my life and a renewal of the sense of purpose that brightens my days on this earth.

THE USE OF PHRASES IN SUSTAINING A VISION

There's one last dimension of choosing a vision I'd like to address in our discussion of this second key to awakening with purpose and joy as we age. It involves the use of pithy phrases that can be recited aloud or referenced internally. These serve as reset buttons for awareness, inviting us into present time, and softening our hearts when we feel emotionally triggered or confused. Each spiritual tradition has its own version of such phrases, and people sometimes make up their own. What matters is the way in which these teachings remind us to gently step out of our unconscious identification with the small self. The phrases become a flashing yellow light on our inner dashboard, reminiscent of the mynah birds in Aldous Huxley's novel *Island*, which would repeatedly call out, "Attention," and "Here and now, boys."

Some of us find great solace in ancient, time-tested teachings of this kind. In the Jewish tradition, the prayer known as the Shema—"the watchword of our people"—serves as an invitation into presence: "Hear, O Israel, the Lord our God, the Lord is one." For Buddhist practitioners, the refuge vows serve a similar purpose, offering people an easily accessible way to return to a source of inner strength and peace: "I take refuge in the Buddha, I take refuge in the Dharma, I take refuge in the Sangha." In the Russian Orthodox tradition of Christianity, the classic nineteenth-century text *The Way of the Pilgrim* teaches the Jesus Prayer, a short formulation that serves to deepen the faith of pilgrims as they experience the inevitable ups and downs of the Way. Their practice is to "pray without ceasing," so they continually recite their prayer: "Lord Jesus Christ, Son of God, have mercy on me, a sinner."

Ram Dass popularized a teaching of this kind that his guru, Neem Karoli Baba (Maharaji), gave him in the late 1960s. He had been studying and practicing yoga intensively at one of Neem Karoli Baba's ashrams in India for a number of months when he found out he had to return to the United States. Aware of how sensitive and vulnerable he felt as a result of the demanding practices he was doing and the simple, quiet lifestyle he was living, Ram Dass felt a great deal of fear and resistance when he thought about going back to the stressful, materialistic West. Before leaving the ashram, he expressed his concerns to Maharaji and asked for guidance that would help with the transition. His teacher said, "Love everyone, serve everyone, and remember God."

I remember when I first heard Ram Dass talk about leaving the ashram and receiving that guidance. That was several decades ago. I felt like I'd been handed a compass that I could use for the rest of my life to find the spiritual equivalent of true north. In the years that followed, I've returned to those three phrases countless times when I feel confused, disheartened, or overwhelmed. Anne Frank said it well: "Look at how a single candle can both defy and define the darkness."

Several years ago, I was fortunate to learn about another teaching of this kind. Angie, a friend from our meditation community in Boulder, had recently returned from a month-long retreat at Spirit Rock Meditation Center in California. I knew it was the first retreat of that length she had attended, and I was curious to hear about her experience. She was happy to tell me about it in detail, and as we were nearing the end of our conversation, she said, "There was one dharma talk that Sally Armstrong, one of the teachers, gave that turned out to be a real high point of the month."

"What was her talk about?" I asked.

"It was about what she called 'the Dharma in six words.'"

The implication was that Sally had captured the essence

of countless volumes of Buddhist wisdom in just six words. At that moment, I felt an intense curiosity. "What were they?" I asked.

Angie paused—to remember the six words or to create suspense, I'm not sure which. "Pay attention; don't cling; be kind."

Those six words immediately became a new touchpoint for me, one that I've found to be extremely helpful on a number of occasions. If I were a person who liked tattoos on my body, I'd have those words tattooed on the inside of my left forearm. As it stands, they're etched on my heart of hearts.

CHAPTER THREE
AWAKENING INTUITION

I didn't arrive at my understanding of the fundamental
laws of the universe through my rational mind.
—ALBERT EINSTEIN

HERE'S A PIECE of good news: we live in a time when an
amazing number of authentic contemplative teachings are
easily accessible to anyone who seeks them out. The not-
so-good news is that there are so many different views and
practice methods that it's easy to become overwhelmed
by the options and end up digging a lot of shallow holes.
Once we've identified our highest intentions and formed a
meaningful vision of what's possible in our lives, how do
we choose methods and perspectives from among this vast
array to support our process of awakening?

A *Wizard of Id* comic strip I came across captures our
current predicament. It shows a medieval peasant walking
down a dirt road. Off in the distance is a castle with a guard
in the watchtower.

"Who goes there?" yells the guard.

The peasant is taken aback. He stops, looks up at the guard, and calls out, "Just a simple pilgrim in search of Nirvana."

The guard responds, "The liquid or the cream?"

The peasant pauses a moment and yells back, "I think I'll be moving on."

How do we know what type of meditation or prayer to practice? How do we decide which book to read? How do we know which teacher we should study with? Is it OK to blend practices, or should we choose one path and stick with it for a long time? What kind of service work should we do? What's the right balance of inner work and activism? How often should we do intensive retreat practice? Which of the many inner voices can we trust to lead us to true freedom?

These questions and others like them inevitably arise for those of us who follow our heart's deepest aspirations. The answers come from a realm of knowing that is often unappreciated in our modern Western society, which tends to be both antimystical and anticontemplative. Intuition is first and foremost *a way of knowing*. It includes the intellect yet goes beyond it. It includes the body, the emotions, and what some people call a "felt sense." It may appear to be irrational at times. It's an innate part of our being that functions like an inner guide, or what Gordon McKeeman, one of my mentors at the Graduate Theological Union, called "an impulse toward wholeness." The Quakers call this natural wisdom the "still, small voice within."[1]

While intuition is difficult to pin down in words, we recognize it when we see it operating in our lives or the lives of others. The following story is one example:

> My father was dying; my mother was panicking. They were three thousand miles away from me. I had a family and a job. And all the familiar questions of these experiences: when to be with them, when to be at home and at work; when to call, when to wait to be called; medical decisions; hospital or home; and simply what to say, how to be.
>
> I'd think and think about all this, but I would reach a point where I'd see I had to stop. My mind would go "tilt." So, I would go out and take a walk, or watch the river change tides and empty into the Atlantic. I'd watch kids at the playground. I'd see how the tree line had changed shape at the top of a mountain meadow I'd known for years. Things like that.
>
> And sometimes I'd hear: "Right. It's time to be out there. I'll leave in two weeks and stay ten days." Or, "Not so much advice giving." Or, "God is with them." The right thought. Something that would ring true. These seemed to come out of the blue, but I felt trust in them, and peaceful as a result.
>
> It was very reliable and very inspiring, working that way. All through his illness and the wild, anxious phone calls, I'd feel answers coming. It was very reassuring. I experienced it as grace. And at the

end I was able to be with them at home and have his hand in mine as he died and my arm around my mother.[2]

Contemplative teachings address the issue of intuitive wisdom quite directly, which makes sense because these traditions are rooted in our fundamental connection with other living beings, the earth, and the cosmos. Intuitive wisdom flows naturally from this interdependent web of reality when we attune to it. Buddhist teachers, for instance, talk about three ways in which we come to understand our true nature and the natural wisdom that arises from it.[3] One is by "hearing the teachings." This could be attending a talk by a spiritual teacher at a meditation group or religious service. It could be listening to a podcast or reading a book by such a teacher. We're introduced to new ways of thinking, which become seeds planted in our mind-stream. In addition, the quality of heartfelt presence some teachers bring to their teaching can serve as a model that amplifies the effects of their words. We recognize and feel uplifted by teachers who convey personal integrity, "walk their talk," and speak truthfully from direct experience.

A second way we come to know our awakened heart-mind is through reflection on the teachings we've received. We begin to examine our own life experience and spiritual practice through these new lenses. Through contemplation and inquiry, we start to make the teachings our own. When we see their truth in our own experience, the "information" we received when hearing the teachings moves to another level of our being. We begin to notice that there are fundamental principles that have been operating in our lives all along. It's as if we're being reminded of something that we already know on the intuitive level. Our understanding deepens, and our trust in the process of awakening deepens along with it.

A third way we come to know reality is through formal training in meditation or prayer. Regardless of the specific methodology, contemplative practices are designed to facilitate direct personal observations, insights, and realizations that are the building blocks of intuition. Rather than thinking about someone else's words and thoughts or reflecting on our own, we are now directly encountering the teachings in our own being and verifying their truth in a uniquely personal way.

While I believe it's impossible to completely capture this kind of intuitive wisdom in words, there are creative and gifted people who come very close to doing so. A poet who comes to mind is Li Po, who lived in eighth-century China:

> The birds have vanished into the sky,
> and now the last cloud drains away.
>
> We sit together, the mountain and me,
> until only the mountain remains.[4]

Note the way this brief poem takes us from an intellectual understanding of oneness to the very edge of intuitive insight. When I read the poem aloud, mindfully and slowly, and then set it aside, I feel as if the confetti of busy-ness that often fills my mind gently settles to the ground in slow motion. My sense of having a personal boundary begins to loosen and dissolve. Try it for yourself and see what happens.

Consider Tony, a fifty-three-year-old computer program-mer who met with me for life coaching on and off over a period of seven years. He was good at what he did, and it paid well, something he brought up regularly in our ses-sions. The problem was that he didn't enjoy his work or find much meaning in it. After bouncing back and forth several times between competitive companies, he came into a ses-sion one day and announced that he'd decided to make a career change. He planned to get a master's degree in edu-cation and teach high school math.

"Let's talk about what led you to make this decision," I said. "I'm curious to know what went on inside you."

"Well, you know better than anyone that I haven't been happy with my work for quite a while. I've been feeling very stuck and yet unwilling to give up the income and lifestyle that come with the job I have. After our session last week, I got a phone call from a friend of mine who told me that Frank, one of the regulars in our golf foursome, had been killed in a car accident. A drunk driver ran a red light and broadsided Frank's car."

His voice slowed and softened when he spoke the last two sentences. I could see from the look on Tony's face that Frank's death had really shaken him to the core. He sat quietly, and I imagined him to be reliving the phone call and the sad reality of how Frank died. I could feel both the shock and the heartache that I saw written on Tony's face.

"Help me connect the dots, Tony," I said. While I thought I knew what he would say, I wanted to hear him say it. More importantly, I wanted *him* to hear himself say it with me bearing witness to his words.

"I just *got it!*" said Tony. "I've been living like I'm going to be here forever, like I have all the time in the world. That's simply not true. I asked myself how much longer I was going to continue programming and what it would take for me to make a change. That's when I remembered Mr. Simpson, my calculus teacher in high school. This guy just loved numbers and what we can do in our world when we know now to use them wisely. His inspiration is what led me to choose math as my major when I went to Cal Berkeley."

Tony looked more alive than I'd seen him look in a long time. "In my mind's eye," he continued, "I saw that I could be someone who taught the way he did, and I imagined myself teaching at my old high school in Santa Barbara. You wouldn't believe how excited I felt. I just knew it was the right next step, and the time to make the change was now, as soon as possible. The strategic part feels easy compared to figuring out what would light up my life while I'm still healthy and able to contribute. That's the puzzle piece that's been missing for so long."

As is clear from this story, the applicability of intuitive wisdom extends far beyond transcendental breakthroughs or esoteric visions. Tony knew on a deeply integrated level that it was time to change careers. In a similar manner, skillful parents develop a kind of "practice wisdom" that helps them decide when to set firm, strong boundaries for their children and when to express their love in a gentle, supportive way. When I did relationship counseling, I noticed the way that longtime intimate partners learned how to "read" what's going on with one another. In healthy relationships, that ability is one of the reasons they remain partners for as long they do. They develop an attunement of which we're all capable when our minds are quiet and our hearts are open.

Once we set foot on the spiritual path, the journey tends to have a life of its own. It's difficult, if not impossible, to reverse course. One way to understand the process is to see it as an ongoing movement from habitual conceptualization to creative intuition. On the most profound level, we are each a compassionate presence through which flows ever-changing streams of phenomena. Because this is so, our understanding will continually evolve as we increasingly recognize the present moment as the heartbeat of reality. All of our questions begin to drop away, and with that, our desperate craving for answers also drops away. Perhaps this is what Buckminster Fuller was referring to when he titled one of his books *I Seem to Be a Verb*.

DISTINGUISHING INTUITION FROM SELF-DECEPTION

I've come to believe that the only human trait as amazing as our intuitive inner guidance is our capacity for self-deception. In this regard, Ram Dass referred to the still, small voice within "surrounded by the trumpets of our desires." This sentiment is echoed in a Taoist teaching: "Truth waits for eyes unclouded by longing."[5]

What happens when we don't effectively distinguish self-deception from authentic intuition? We can easily convince ourselves that we're seeing reality clearly when what we're actually doing is living in a fantasy world of our own creation. Consider the following example from a meditation retreat Ram Dass attended.

> I was taking a meditation course once, and I arrived five minutes after the course began. You go in silence; you're not allowed to talk to anyone else during the course. I had a roommate, and he was very neat; he did hospital corners on his bed. I decided he didn't like me—that I was a slob and he didn't like me. I spent all week staying out of the room because I felt he didn't like me. I figured I might snore, maybe that was it. But I just got a feeling that he was so clean and neat that he couldn't like somebody like me. I built up this incredible feeling that this guy hated me. When the course was over, he walked up to me and said, "I want to introduce myself and tell you that just knowing I was in the same room as you and sharing this with you helped my meditation so much. Thank you. I felt so much love for you. I wish I could have told you."

I suddenly saw my mind. I had created this

incredible mountain of paranoia and spent a whole
week worrying about it. And it was all in my mind.[6]

Because he was in a retreat environment, Ram Dass was
able to see and appreciate the delusory nature of this experience as a powerful teaching, one that he could embrace
with perspective and humor. It's a fine example of the kind
of mind dynamic a meditation retreat is intended to illumi-
nate. This is the same basic process that a lot of us notice
in our daily lives time and time again. We think we're seeing reality clearly and that we can trust our intuition about
what's happening, when in truth what we're seeing are projections of our own minds.

Frequently, our projections are rooted in our feelings of
desire, aversion, and confusion, in relation to both ourselves and others. The Pali word *vipassana* is sometimes
translated as "insight," as when we talk about insight meditation. Two other common translations of vipassana are
informative here: "seeing things as they are" and "seeing
things clearly." When we're seeing clearly and attending to
our intuitive inner guidance, the process can feel breath-
taking, even magical.

As I mentioned in chapter 1, in the spring of 1984 I was
working as the director of the Mesilla Valley Hospice in Las
Cruces, New Mexico. Having originally been hired as a con-
sultant for a six-month period, I had extended my stay with
the intention of helping this fledgling organization get certified as a home health agency and hospice program. The
two certifications would significantly increase the finan-

cial viability of these programs and the likelihood that they would take root in the Las Cruces community. The board of directors had recently asked me to stay on permanently as the director of the hospice program. I felt intense ambivalence about the offer, both wanting to take the position and wanting to leave Las Cruces to start a new chapter of my life.

Rather than force myself to make a decision when I wasn't feeling ready to do so, I decided to use my vacation time to go on retreat at St. Benedict's Monastery in Colorado. I had been to the monastery several times before and had always found it to be a refuge that allowed me to slow down and listen to my innermost being.

The first night in the monastery guest house, I had two dreams. In the first one, I descended a staircase and entered a completely dark basement. Wandering around in the dark was the perfect metaphor for how I felt about the hospice decision. I just couldn't "see" what felt right. I reached out my hands and made contact with a wall, and at that point I had the thought that woke me up: *I don't know if I'm coming or going.* I literally didn't know if I was outside a room trying to break in or inside a room trying to break out. The feeling of bewilderment stayed with me for a long time after I awoke from the dream. It was still the middle of the night, so I did my best to relax, hoping I would fall back to sleep.

When I did, I had another dream. In the second dream, I remembered my vision from three years earlier when I initially met Father Thomas Keating. I reconnected with the feeling of having to choose who would be my mother:

my actual mother or Mother Mary. At first I struggled, and then, as my body and mind settled, the decision became crystal clear. I would once again choose Mother Mary. She had already chosen me when I first visited the monastery. I would turn down the position with Mesilla Valley Hospice. That's when I woke up.

It took a couple of days for me to articulate what I had understood. Eventually, the words came to me, and I was able to journal about what I had realized. The appearance of my mother represented my psychological identity. I knew that my mother was quite proud of the fact that I was directing a service organization involving physicians, nurses, and other health professionals while still only thirty-four years old. The part of me that wanted to keep the job wanted to do so in part to please my mother and in part to "look good" in a society that cared a lot about status and power. The part of me that wanted to choose Mother Mary understood that to awaken to the true nature of who I am and who we all are, I needed to disidentify with my psychological identity and the merit badges associated with it. Instead, I needed to become a child of the spirit for whom life is mysterious, profound, and often uncertain.

When I wrote about my experience, it clearly felt right. I also spoke to some close friends who listened thoughtfully. In hearing myself describe the dreams to them and the insights that followed, I felt complete trust in my decision. The dream symbols were clear, and I knew what to do. I returned to Las Cruces and told the board what I had decided, which they accepted graciously.

The ability to distinguish authentic intuitive wisdom from self-deception that is rooted in the needs of the ego is something we can all develop. In the same way that we can learn to distinguish food that is nutritious from food that contains nothing but empty calories, we can learn to recognize which inner voices are trustworthy and which are leading us astray. Martha Crampton, a psychologist with a transpersonal orientation, offers us some helpful guidelines for cultivating this kind of discrimination.[7]

As a starting point, Crampton recommends that we pay close attention to our motivation. The more altruistic the intention we bring to a given decision, the greater the likelihood that wise inner guidance will play a role. Living in accordance with basic ethical guidelines and embracing a lifestyle that is nonharming further supports the person who aspires to tap into their deepest inner wisdom and compassion.

Crampton points out that authentic inner guidance often brings with it a feeling of calmness, certainty, and resolution—assuming we have sufficient receptivity and inner stillness to let those feelings in. This is even true of difficult or inconvenient messages that a part of us doesn't want to hear. It's best to be skeptical of messages that either greatly flatter us or predict disaster. Such extreme messages are usually rooted in the unconscious. In the case of flattery, they typically represent a compensatory response associated with low self-esteem. Warnings of disaster are often due to neurotic guilt that creates a belief that we deserve to suffer. It can be helpful to use the power of reason to evaluate our intuitive impressions, although we need to be cautious not to make reason the sole arbiter of our decisions.

There are several other points to consider in authenticating our intuitions. Sometimes these impressions come in symbolic form. In my own life, for example, I've learned that when I'm avoiding conflict and storing up angry feelings, I often dream about packs of wild dogs. If the feelings are closer to rage than ordinary anger, I dream about sharks. On some level, I associate sharks with aggression that is devoid of anything that can be controlled or modified. Dreams of this kind sometimes tip me off that my anger about a recent event is being amplified by a similar unfinished experience from the past.

Each of us has a unique symbolic vocabulary, and with training we can become increasingly aware of the way the unconscious and conscious aspects of the mind communicate with each another. The many methods of tapping into the unconscious that have been developed in humanistic and transpersonal psychology offer us excellent tools. Art therapy, imagery work, music therapy, psychodrama, dance and movement therapy, deep bodywork, and dreamwork all have the potential to contribute to the cultivation and refinement of inner guidance.

When there's a lack of clarity about a decision, it's helpful to hit the pause button and engage in what Martha Crampton calls a period of "cold storage." Pausing decision making strengthens our tolerance for uncertainty and gives our intuition time to develop. Lao Tzu describes this process in the Tao Te Ching:

Do you have the patience to wait
till your mud settles and the water is clear?
Can you remain unmoving
till the right action arises by itself?[8]

Another skillful means to consider is checking out your intuitions with people you trust and know well, as I did with friends in the wake of my dreams at St. Benedict's. Your advisor might be a respected and longtime friend, a mentor at work, a wise teacher, a grandparent, or a counselor. It should be someone familiar with what you bring to the situation and with the issues involved. The same is true of groups of people who may be able to assist. Perhaps you've been in a personal growth group, a spiritual study group, or a twelve-step group with the same people for many years. This may be another fruitful opportunity to ask for feedback about a decision you're contemplating.

In the end, Crampton encourages us to return to where we started—purifying our motivation so we can align ourselves with our highest intentions. I heard a story about the Dalai Lama being interviewed by a reporter. He was asked about the demands of being on the world stage and making decisions that affected large numbers of Tibetans and other people around the world. "Your Holiness," the reporter asked, "how do you know you're doing the right thing?" The Dalai Lama thought for a moment and said, "My pure intention is my protection."

INTUITION AND THE TWO TRUTHS

Exploring the meaning and value of intuition leads many
people to see why it plays such a central role in the movement toward spiritual liberation. Because it involves a new
and different way of knowing ourselves, each other, and our
world, intuitive wisdom radically transforms the way we
live. It reveals secrets that have been here all along but have
remained unrecognized. Perhaps this is what Antoine de
Saint-Exupéry was referring to in his classic book *The Little
Prince* when he wrote, "Here is my secret. It's quite simple:
One sees clearly only with the heart. Anything essential is
invisible to the eyes."[9]

To take our discussion of intuition to the deeper spiritual
territory indicated, we have to understand the difference
between *conceptualization* and *realization*. I got a clear look
at this distinction the first time I attended a silent ten-day
meditation retreat at the Insight Meditation Society in
Massachusetts. I was thirty years old and had been practicing yoga and meditation for about nine years. I'd read and
thought a lot about "living in the present" and believed I
had attained a certain understanding and level of mastery
in that regard. The retreat schedule was rigorous, much
more demanding than that of the relaxing yoga retreats I
had attended previously.

As the long days of intensive meditation practice accu-
mulated, my concentration became very strong. Like a
flashlight that was ultrabright, it enabled me to see with
exquisite precision how much time I actually spent "lost

in thought" and how rarely my body and mind were in the same place at the same time.

This was particularly evident at the silent meals we retreatants shared. I slowed down a great deal and gave my complete attention to the act of eating in a way that I had never done before. Doing so led to a surprisingly powerful revelation. Not only did the food look and taste amazing, but there were also frequent moments in which the flow of time seemed to stop. There was no separation between me as a subject and the food as an object. Rather, there was just the process of eating, with no conscious purpose or effort. That's when I understood that living in the present involved the dissolution of the sense of a separate self and the realization of what Buddhist teachings call "nonduality."

The notion of nonduality, or what some teachings call "unitive consciousness," is something that many people understand intellectually. In the modern ecology movement, we see many examples of the interdependence of all life on earth. Modern physics tells us that energy cannot be created or destroyed, only converted from one form to another. Such logic and evidence enable us to embrace the idea of oneness and inspire us to look more deeply at its implications. When we do, we see that unity expresses itself on two fundamental levels: the absolute and the relative. My Tibetan teachers called these the two truths and used the terms *ultimate* and *conventional*, respectively, when they talked about them.

The relative level is the level of our humanness and our individual differences. It's the infinite level of unique forms that express the basic life force that enlivens and connects us all. The absolute level is variously described as the realm of unity, Tao, emptiness, the Eternal Now, or the Divine. Experientially, it's a dynamic, interconnected web from which all apparently separate manifestations arise. Thich Nhat Hanh used the image of the ocean to illustrate the relationship between these two aspects of life. He distinguished the profound stillness at the bottom of the ocean floor from the roiling waves on the surface and pointed out that they are both expressions of the same vast body of water. While the waves that rise and fall appear to be temporarily distinct from one another, they always arise from and return to a common source.

A conceptual understanding of unitive consciousness is extremely helpful and often leads us to significantly deepen our commitment to conscious living. A direct experience of nonduality, however, goes far beyond *ideas* about who we are as individuals and the nature of reality. I've had the privilege to work with a number of people who have reported breakthroughs that radically changed their understanding of themselves and the world. A participant at a retreat I taught in the mountains of Colorado wrote to me after returning home and shared this delightful example:

> A glimpse? On silent retreat two weeks ago, during a period of walking meditation, a sudden fluttering appeared in front of my face. A hummingbird. I became so instantly still not even my pupils shifted to focus on what was happening. After a moment

it flew up close, into my beard, and was poking
around on my chin. Gentle, yet firm, and with the
same pressure each time. Then it pulled back,
paused, and went right up my left nostril. It poked
around up there five or six times and again pulled
back and paused before going up my right nostril.
Up until that moment I'd had no thought. Total
stillness. Awareness was experiencing the process I
call hummingbird as not separate from the totality,
as awareness was also not separate. After a couple
of pokes up the right nostril, a thought: will it move
up to poke my eye? In this moment the hummingbird moved back, took one last look, and flew away.
I imagined when "I" wondered if "it" was going to
poke "my" eye, a thin layer of identity and separateness had been created, leaving "me" in awe.[10]

Where does this process of awakening intuition lead us?
It enables us to see the inherent sacredness and seamless-
ness of our lives, whether we're paying bills, caring for children, repeating ancient mantras, mowing the lawn, working
at a bank, or practicing meditation in a remote mountain
hermitage. One activity is not better than the other, and
there's no need whatsoever to be anywhere except where
we are to do what needs to be done.

We come to understand that it's primarily the quality of
consciousness we bring to our activity that determines its
effect on our lives and the lives of those with whom we come
into contact. The intentional cultivation of mindfulness

and compassion, by whatever skillful means we deem appropriate, actualizes our profound potential for knowing who and what we really are and for looking deeply into the ultimate mystery that we each embody in our own unique way. While we can never "know" this mystery as something apart from ourselves, we can merge into it to become a living expression of its inherent goodness.

CHAPTER FOUR
COMMITTING TO INNER WORK

To know thyself is the beginning of wisdom.

—SOCRATES

ONE OF OUR fundamental tasks as spiritual practitioners is to open fully to the truth of living in a human body. Where else but in our bodies can we encounter and cultivate the wise intuition discussed in the previous chapter? Yet for all sorts of reasons, staying present and awake to our bodies is a challenging task. Part of us wants to commit to the inner work of spiritual realization—the fourth key to awakening with purpose and joy as we age—and we know we have to face our bodily existence to do so. Easier said than done. The physical experiences that arise in our lives run the gamut from intense pleasure to intense pain, with stops along the entire spectrum between the two.

A lot of us tend to disown our bodies, treating them like objects we'd rather not deal with. Many of us struggle with feelings of shame and inadequacy in this regard, aware that we'll never meet our own expectations, let alone those popularized by the media. It's as if we're living in a rented apartment we really dislike, yet we can't find any viable means of escape.

James Joyce captured our predicament when he described a character in one of his short stories this way: "[Mr. Duffy] lived a little distance from his body."[1] There seems to be a Mr. or Ms. Duffy in each of us. While it's true that there's more to who we are than our physical selves, a necessary step in understanding that "more" is fully inhabiting our bodies. To do so, we must remain attuned to our physicality and not excessively desensitize ourselves to avoid the inevitable sensations and feelings that are part of being human.

This aspect of awakening becomes increasingly poignant as we grow older and are forced to acknowledge our physical limitations. The knees that once took us on long jogs now ache after sitting too long in a chair. Looking in the mirror, we see a person who looks a little rounder, a little more wrinkled, or a lot grayer than we expected. What makes all the difference when we work with these issues is the vision we talked about in chapter 2, the way we understand who we are and what we're on earth to do. We can unconsciously embrace the modern social lament that aging is bad news and bound to get worse over time. This approach lends itself to frequent complaining—internally, to others, or both. To wake up from this trance, we must learn to distinguish healthy self-compassion from victim-oriented self-pity.

When wisely understood, the bodily changes inherent in the aging process become stepping-stones on the road to liberation. They remind us of the aspect of our being that is a part of nature, and they motivate us to look more deeply at the ultimate dimension of who and what we are. This is a process of loving awareness that lives outside conventional time and space.

Sister Ann, a member of a Christian religious order, described her experience of living in an aging body with these words:

> The diminishments of old age school us in the art of humility and self-acceptance. . . . Because we can't rely on our former attainments and on our physical strength, we must search more deeply within ourselves for a fund of inner strength and wisdom. Increased reflection and contemplation in elderhood, as taught by the world's mystical traditions, are invaluable in helping us befriend our hidden depths.[2]

One way we avoid living in our bodies is by shutting down our senses. Each of us has unique habitual patterns of attending to certain stimuli and avoiding others. Some people are highly visual and barely notice the sounds in their inner and outer environments. Others are quite attuned to auditory experience and pay minimal attention to the visual aspect of the world. Still others, such as gourmet cooks, have developed their awareness of taste and smell to a high degree. Then there are those whose sense of taste is quite dull and accompanied by a similar limitation in the sense of smell. These individual differences are best understood as being just what they are—individual differences. Comparing ourselves to one another is unhelpful and often quite painful.

We can see the effect of habitual desensitization in a psychotherapist's description of a session with a longtime client:

> When she first came to see me, this woman hadn't been speaking for three months. But she was silent in many different ways. Resentful silence: "You do it for me." Agitated silence: "I'm scared." Bored silence: "I have nothing." A kind of interested silence too—but not knowing how to start. After several months she began to speak.
>
> Now, after a number of years, she spends a great deal of time talking, and she's afraid of silence, scared of being quiet. There are things, she says, that she doesn't want to know. Any movement into silence, from outside or within, is really frightening.
>
> One day there was a noise outside. She paused and said, "What's that?" I said, "Let's listen." She listened for a moment and asked again, "What is it?" I said again, "Let's listen." And then she exclaimed, with total delight, "It's a bird! I haven't heard a bird in years. It's beautiful!" I saw it all go by: the noise, the not knowing (imagine the condition of one who doesn't know the sound of a bird!), her wish to hear,

the listening, the sound recognized, the bird. There was another long silence. Then she said, "That's just so beautiful!"[3]

This woman's experience is somewhat extreme, possibly indicative of trauma in her past. But the Mr. or Ms. Duffy in each of us maintains a fixed set of habits and preferences concerning which sensations are noticeable and acceptable, and which are not. Some of us have made the aperture of sensation so narrow that we hardly notice anything besides crude pleasures and pains. Others have significantly heightened their kinesthetic awareness and are constantly refining their sensory knowledge of the world.

When I was training as a yoga teacher in my early twenties, I met people who were amazingly attuned to the subtlest of bodily sensations. Some of these people attended to their physical experience and used it as a significant source of information to feed their intuition. They often used language that referred to their bodies: "My gut told me to take the job in Boston even though the salary was smaller than that of the job in Los Angeles." "As much as I didn't want to face it, my heart made it clear to me that it was time to end the relationship." "As soon as I walked into the room, I noticed a feeling in the pit of my stomach that told me this was not a safe situation."

Some people I've worked with over the years are clearly in touch with and deeply interested in sexual feelings. Others repress, ignore, or redirect them, in some cases intentionally training themselves to focus their attention elsewhere.

Those of us who have unhealed physical or sexual trauma in our history may find it hard to be on the earth at all, let alone to be comfortable in our own skin. In the following example, Buddhist teacher Jack Kornfield shows us how a willingness to bring caring and focused attention to our deep yearnings can lead to valuable self-understanding:

In my earliest practice as a celibate monk I had long bouts of lust and images of sexual fantasy. My teacher said to name them, which I did. But they often repeated. "Accept this?" I thought. "But then they'll never stop." But still I tried it. Over days and weeks these thoughts became even stronger. Eventually, I decided to expand my awareness to see what other feelings were present. To my surprise I found a deep well of loneliness almost every time the fantasies arose. It wasn't all lust, it was loneliness, and the sexual images were ways of seeking comfort and closeness. But they kept arising. Then I noticed how hard it was to let myself feel the loneliness. I hated it; I resisted it. Only when I accepted this very resistance and gently held it all in compassion did it begin to subside. By expanding the attention, I learned that much of my sexuality had little to do with lust, and as I brought an acceptance to the feeling of loneliness, the compulsive quality of the fantasies gradually diminished.[4]

This recognition of the necessity of embodiment applies to every aspect of our journey. Even what sometimes gets labeled as an enlightenment experience or a moment of God-realization is only transformational when it's integrated into a person's embodied life. Otherwise, it simply becomes an uplifting moment that brings little benefit to the world other than the temporary good mood of the person experiencing such a state. What's essential is that we learn to distinguish *thinking about* the teachings from *living* the teachings on the level of felt experience. From the poet Kabir:

> There is nothing but water in the holy pools.
> I know, I have been swimming in them.
> All the gods sculpted of wood or ivory can't say a word.
> I know, I have been crying out to them.
> The Sacred Books of the East are nothing but words.
> I looked through their covers one day sideways.
> What Kabir talks of is only what he has lived through.
> If you have not lived through something, it is not true.[5]

The point is not that we should be perfectly aware of every single physical sensation and sense impression in every waking moment. That's not possible even for the most advanced and highly concentrated practitioners of hatha yoga, tai chi, or aikido. It's also not the case that we should criticize ourselves when we notice the ways in which we've temporarily shut down on the physical level. Rhythms of expansion and contraction are built in to how we function as human beings. Rather, the point is to acknowledge that, on one plane of existence, we are physical beings who can learn to recognize the inherent goodness and beauty of our embodied nature, just as it is, in any given moment.

Why is this wholehearted ownership of our physical bodies such an important aspect of our inner work? It's because our bodies are natural gateways to our deeper nature that reveal essential principles of reality. What we come to realize is that when we pay close enough attention to anything, we will see its sacredness. This is the attitude that supports our inquiry into who we are as physical beings and who we are *in addition to* physical beings. Such a spirit of investigation energizes the entire process of awakening. In the early stages, we need to pay attention intentionally to the richness of our humanness as we gradually and simultaneously learn to inhabit our transcendent nature. The Christian mystic Meister Eckhart described this process when he said, "Let God be God in you."[6]

Just as we all have habitual ways of attending to physical sensations and sense impressions, the same is true of the ways we attend to emotions, moods, and thoughts. Committing to our inner work includes acknowledging and welcoming these experiences as well.

Growing up in a family in which expressing emotions was frowned upon as "rocking the boat," I learned from an early age to limit my expression of emotion to a narrow range of intensity. Any movement beyond that invisible boundary would elicit one of a few painfully familiar phrases: "Don't upset your father," "Don't talk to me that way, young man!" or "Why don't you go and watch some TV?" The message was clear: emotions, especially strong emotions, were problematic and not welcome in our home. I often felt ashamed for simply *having* feelings. Anger, in particular, was completely unacceptable. Without knowing it was happening, I learned to tighten various muscles to restrain myself from expressing anger. With no external outlet, I often directed anger inward in the form of self-criticism, which contributed to low self-esteem and, at times, depression.

For those of us who aspire to live fully and love well, our emotions need to be thoroughly explored and embraced. Doing so doesn't necessarily mean acting out those emotions, although there are certainly skillful ways to express our feelings and appropriate settings in which to do so. Exploring and embracing means opening to what arises and meeting any emotion we experience with friendliness or what I call "loving curiosity."

I first heard this phrase in a classroom at Naropa University after I had led an experiential partner exercise in a course I was teaching. "I'm interested in any feedback you might have about this exercise. What was that like?" I asked. One student put her hand up and paused for a moment after I called on her. "I felt such a sense of loving curiosity when we did the exercise," she said. There was a tenderness in her voice that conveyed awe and openheartedness. It struck me at that moment that she was putting words to an experience I had also had in moments of presence.

We can learn to turn toward what is happening on the emotional level just as we can lean into what happens on the level of physical sensations and sense impressions. By bringing awareness to our bodies and emotions and opening the "sense doors," as they're called in Buddhist teachings, we begin to understand what it means to make friends with ourselves. We start to see that nothing whatsoever is outside of our practice. This process can be quite challenging and we will sometimes feel a strong desire to avoid or resist what is happening. It feels natural for us to turn away from discomfort of any kind. Still, when we are committed to waking up, we come to see that working with resistance to uncomfortable emotions is an essential skill that yields valuable psychological and spiritual insights. Tibetan Buddhists call this "turning poison into medicine."

Heather was a student who took several classes I taught in the transpersonal psychology program at Naropa University. After she graduated and moved away, she sent periodic e-mails to keep me abreast of her life and career path. The following is an excerpt from one of her communications:

> I thought of you this morning. I have been unemployed—unexpectedly—for over a month now and have been active in trying to find work. It's been a great challenge and I have been feeling waves of rejection and doubt, amidst faith and trust. This morning I felt anger arise when I received an e-mail that a company I was hoping to work with had offered the job I was seeking to another person.

COMMITTING TO INNER WORK | 93

I felt cheated and lied to, and very quickly a story unfolded about betrayal and injustice—quick and hot. Then I went to meditate. I was curious about my anger; it felt strong, uncomfortable, and amidst this emotion, oddly enough, I perceived an opportunity. So, I sat. I felt heat and constriction in my chest and a long story that I eventually let go of. And then sadness welled over me and I was in tears with a deep sense of rejection, and again a story that I swung in and out of. Tears and a heaviness in my chest and back followed, and I let myself just cry for a while, no story, just tears. Then . . . came space. No anger, no sadness, just space, quiet, and the storm had passed and it seemed the energy had moved through me and I was just sitting there and everything was sitting there with me and it was quiet . . . That's when I thought of you. Just wanted to share. It was nice to see you in this place and I felt gratitude for practice, for unearthing layers and being with. Thank you.

At the time Heather sent this e-mail, she had been meditating for several years. The fruit of her practice is clearly evident in her willingness to do the inner work, to face her shadow material and "have tea with the demons." We see this in her choice to turn toward instead of away from her anger. As she put it, "I was curious about my anger; it felt strong, uncomfortable, and amidst this emotion, oddly enough, I perceived an opportunity." Rather than resist what was happening and distract herself, she gave her full attention to the outrage she felt and was able to glimpse her true nature, which was the vast space of loving awareness in which she was riding the emotional rapids. In the end, she came to rest in a place of simple presence, a place of peace: "and the storm had passed and it seemed the energy had moved through me and I was just sitting there and everything was sitting there with me and it was quiet."

There's a saying I heard when I was living in Nepal in the 1980s: "The world is like a grinding stone. Either it will grind you up, or it will turn you into something beautiful." I revisit this saying on a regular basis, especially when I'm struggling or hurting. So far in this chapter, we've looked at the importance of being able to turn toward our bodily sensations and emotions. In one sense, learning to do so makes life richer and more real. But we are also training for inevitable times of great intensity—am I prepared to turn toward sensation and emotion as I move through the grinding stone?

Whether we are ground up or turned into something beautiful depends on how we respond to what happens in our lives. More often than not, we have a limited amount of control over the inner and outer events that affect us. In some cases, we have no control whatsoever. On the other hand, we have a lot to say about how we respond to what happens. The many forms of contemplative training we find in the world's wisdom traditions teach us to turn toward the difficulties that arise and to move through their center to the extent to which we're able. It's this kind of movement, which at first seems counterintuitive, that often yields a new and life-changing insight into our true nature and the nature of reality. In the words of the religious scholar and mystic Andrew Harvey,

> Spiritual life has nothing to do with evading suffering. It has everything to do with opening to the full effects of suffering, and by that wild act of opening to suffering—not only in our own lives but in the lives of every being around us—by that act, discovering the mystery of the presence in and beyond suffering. This takes courage; this takes an absolute honesty; this takes a ferocious commitment to truth.[7]

The inner work of becoming intimate with our own bodies, hearts, and minds plays a foundational role in the process of spiritual maturation. Said another way, it is through fully embracing our human vulnerability as it actually is, suffering and all, that we discover our innate capacity for *self-transcendence*. By "minding our own mind-stream," as Zen teacher Yvonne Rand once put it, we enter the primordial ocean of awareness and love that connects all beings across time and space.

The Zen Buddhist teacher Roshi Joan Halifax described just such an experience she had while grieving the death of her mother:

When my mother died, I received one of the hardest and most precious teachings of my entire life. I realized that I only had this one chance to grieve her death. I felt like I had a choice. On the one hand, I could be a so-called "good Buddhist," accept impermanence, and let go of my mother with great dignity. The other alternative was to scour my heart out with honest sorrow.

I chose to scour. After her death, I went to the desert with photographs of her and letters she had written my father after I was born. Settling under a rocky ledge, I sank back into shadows of sorrow. When your mother dies, so does the womb that gave birth to you. I felt that my back was uncovered and exposed even as I pressed it into cold, solid rock. Later, I walked the Himalayas with a friend who had recently lost his mother, too. The autumn rains washed down the mountains and streaked down our wet faces.

When my friend and I arrived in Kathmandu, the lamas there offered to perform a Tibetan ceremony for my mother. They instructed me not to cry but to let her be in peace. By this time, I felt ready to hear their words, and I did not have to force myself to stop mourning. When I let myself drop all the way through to the bottom, I found that my mother had become an ancestor. As I finally released her, she became part of me. And my sadness became part of the river of grief that pulses deep inside us, hidden from view but informing our lives at every turn.[8]

Wary of the cul-de-sac of "spiritual bypassing"—a term coined by Buddhist psychologist John Welwood—Roshi Joan chose not to leapfrog over her grief in the name of pseudospiritual equanimity. She had the trust, courage, and wisdom to surrender to her feelings of loss. Intense as the emotional pain was, she gave herself to it and passed through its center. While this is not an easy thing to do, it's a choice that any one of us can make at any time. If we truly want to live fully and love well during our limited time on earth, we must recognize the fact that the suffering of turning away from reality is ultimately greater than the suffering of surrendering to what is.

THE PRACTICE OF SKILLFUL MEANS

A question that often arises when I talk about committing to inner work involves the actual how-to aspect of it. Once we acknowledge that this fourth key plays an important role in our unfolding journey, we have to make choices of the kind we discussed at the beginning of chapter 3. It's funny on one level to think about nirvana in terms of "the liquid or the cream." Yes, that's how absurd techniques and belief systems can sometimes become. At the same time, it's still true that most of us need to make wise use of transformative practices and perspectives if we want to actualize our innate potential to live wisely and love well.

Let's begin by examining methods and practices in general. Buddhist teacher Gil Fronsdal talks about what he calls "the path of cultivation." This approach emphasizes the developmental dimension of the path and uses the language of growth, development, and self-improvement. We observe ourselves changing from less compassionate to more compassionate, from less concentrated to more concentrated, from less generous to more generous, and from less ethical to more ethical. For many of us in modern Western cultures, this approach keeps us motivated and adds to the meaning of what we're doing day by day. We find it satisfying and energizing when we can see and feel the fruits of our efforts.

There's another side to this coin, however. Living in a culture that so heavily emphasizes productivity and achievement, we're at risk of turning our spiritual practices into psychological accomplishments that boost our self-esteem in a way that leads to unhelpful striving. When this happens, our very efforts to attain spiritual freedom reinforce the ego-identity that liberation is specifically designed to deconstruct. This is the shadow side of the path of cultivation. We can get caught in what Hindu teachings call "the golden chain," a version of spiritual perfectionism in which we become strongly identified with our particular form of practice. We push ourselves to practice as purely and vigorously as possible, hoping for maximum results. Ironically, the methods themselves entrap rather than free us, and we simply add one more layer of ego-identification to the contracted self.

An alternative approach that Fronsdal discusses is called "the pathless path." It functions in a way that avoids the creation of the "spiritual superego" just described. The emphasis in this approach is on the innate aspect of our basic goodness or true nature. Rather than exerting ourselves to try to give birth to a new, improved version of ourselves, we're taught to relax the deeply conditioned impulse to remake ourselves as better, more lovable people. We learn methods and views that focus on self-acceptance, spaciousness, ease, and presence. By resting in things as they are and not creating a sense of struggle, we allow the obstructions that impede expression of our natural wisdom and love to dissolve slowly. I love the description of this process as the clouds parting and gradually disappearing so the brilliant sunlight of our true nature can shine out into the world.

Here again, however, we need to be mindful of a potential problem. Pathless path teachings tell us we already have what we seek, there's nothing to accomplish, and this very moment is the elusive enlightenment we've been chasing. However true that might be on the ultimate level, it's common for people to misunderstand these teachings as saying that no effort is required *at all*. This can lead to complacency rather than the intended spaciousness and sense of flow that we see in highly realized people. It can also lead to disengagement from the very real and urgent political, social justice, and environmental issues that require our care and attention.

I've come to see the path of cultivation and the pathless

path as expressions of a fundamental paradox. It's one that all of us who look deeply at our own lives eventually encounter, that of *being* and *becoming*.[9] Like all paradoxes, this one cannot be grasped by the rational mind with its either-or thinking. What's needed is a "both-and" approach of the intuitive heart-mind and, in some cases, an "all-of-the-above" viewpoint that sees all models and views yet doesn't embrace any of them in an exclusive manner. From this perspective, we discover that we can be grounded in groundlessness. This is the eventual culmination of our inner work. Similarly, in another great paradox of our spiritual unfolding, we will find that the optimal strategy for "making progress" is to practice as if doing so is an end in itself.

What are the practical implications of these seemingly conflicting models of the spiritual path? One implication is that motivation *really* matters. The same methods and perspectives can either reinforce or deconstruct the solidity of the small self, depending on the inner attitude with which they are used. We need to remember that our inner work is in service to our own well-being *and* for the purpose of helping us to be instruments of well-being in the world. We see this in the words of Saint Francis when he says, "Lord, make me an instrument of your peace." It is likewise apparent in the words of Buddhist practitioners who dedicate the merit associated with their practice to the benefit of all living beings without exception.

When we shift to a both-and perspective, we can see that there may be times when it's appropriate to choose the path of cultivation. This is particularly true for those of us who are new to meditation, prayer, and similar practices. Creating life-affirming, prosocial habits involves a learning curve and initially, for many people, an uphill climb. There may be times in our lives when we need small goals more than grand visions. We might think in terms of managing angry feelings more effectively with family members, being more generous with strangers, or simply being kinder toward ourselves. Seeing progress in areas like these encourages us to stay on the path and to weather the periodic difficulties that require us to really stretch.

At other times, we may notice that our practice is feeling rote, lifeless, dutiful. Or we may be ruminating in a self-critical manner, wrestling with feelings of shame, guilt, or inadequacy. Maintaining our commitment to practice at times like these can bear life-changing fruit if we gain insight into the confused perceptions and beliefs that fuel the patterns involved. Pathless path teachings slow us down, deepen our breathing, and remind us to settle back into the present moment as our reference point for ultimate reality. They encourage us to take our foot off the accelerator and coast a while as we move through whatever temporary experience is manifesting. Over time, as we integrate the natural ease of the pathless path and the wise effort of the path of cultivation, we are gradually blessed with a deep faith in ourselves and in life as a whole.

This is not conventional faith in the sense of a theological belief system that we're told we simply have to accept. Rather, we come to understand that the word *faith* can be understood in a variety of ways, one of which is "trusting our own deepest experience."[10] In the next chapter, we'll come to see why this kind of faith, this profound sense of trust, is so beneficial and so critically important.

CHAPTER FIVE

SUFFERING EFFECTIVELY

There are two kinds of suffering: the suffering that
leads to more suffering and the suffering that leads to
the end of suffering. If you are not willing to face the
second kind of suffering, you will surely continue to
experience the first.

—AJAHN CHAH

WHEN I TEACH "Aging and Awakening" workshops, I often
begin with an exercise designed to break the ice and intro-
duce the essence of the workshop. I ask the participants to
divide up into groups of three, creating small circles in which
they can talk easily. I then say some version of, "This is an
exercise called 'power whining.' Most of us have been taught
from an early age that complaining is to be avoided at all
costs. As my mother used to say, 'Nobody likes a complainer.'
We've been told complaining is unhelpful to ourselves and
unattractive to others, a behavior that people find irritat-
ing or worse. For the five minutes that we do this exercise,
we're going to suspend this prohibition of complaining and

give ourselves total permission to complain to our heart's content. In fact, once I let you know what I'd like you to complain about, I'd like you to *exaggerate* your complaints. Make them even larger than they are in real life."

The responses to this instruction are usually a blend of mumbled groans, rolling eyes, and people looking at the floor or their watch. I can see them worrying about what they've gotten themselves into, perhaps even wondering how to leave the workshop early. "Here's what I'd like you to talk about in your small group. I want you to complain about all the aspects of aging you don't like. Remember, for these five minutes, it's completely OK to complain. I'm asking you to really lean into your complaints, be theatrical if you'd like to. Is the instruction clear? Any questions? . . . OK, let's begin." Then I ring a meditation bell and start the timer on my watch.

The room slowly comes alive. At first, I hear low voices cautiously muttering one- or two-word complaints. Then, after a minute or so, the pace and volume pick up significantly, and pockets of laughter erupt in various parts of the room. By the third minute, the voices become quite loud, even musical in a certain sense. I close my eyes and listen to them the way I would listen to the sounds of a rainforest or a waterfall. At four minutes, I turn my microphone back on and call out to the participants, "You have one minute left to share your complaints." By now, most of them are feeling quite bonded to the other people in their small group, and they don't want to stop. The laughter has gotten progressively louder, and I have to decide how to get people to *stop* sharing their complaints. I then tell them it's time to stop, ringing a bell intermittently until the room becomes quiet. "Please take a moment to acknowledge the people in your group in whatever way feels appropriate and then return your chairs to where they were before we did the exercise."

Then I "harvest" responses, asking people to call out some of the complaints they spoke or heard in their groups. There's a short silence, and then one brave person starts the feedback: "Memory problems." Just as at the start of the exercise, the pace picks up quickly. "Feeling invisible." "Poor sleep." "Low energy level." "Side effects from medications." "Frequent urination." "Losing my reading glasses . . . and then finding them on my forehead." "Friends dying." "Decreased libido." "Poor night vision." "Loneliness." Various heads nod with each response, and people become bolder and more vulnerable as the process continues.

Silent gaps begin to arise before additional comments are made. Eventually the feedback peters out, and the room becomes still. "Notice how you're feeling right now," I say. "No need to criticize yourself or your feelings. Be a compassionate witness. Simply pay attention to your emotions, thoughts, mood—what are you noticing?" Again, responses pop up from various parts of the room: "Depressed." "Afraid." "Sad." "Angry." "Helpless." "Frustrated." "Hopeless." There's a palpable heaviness in the environment now. I let the silence and somberness linger for a time as I study the faces of the people in the group before speaking again.

"I think it's important from the outset that we don't sugarcoat the challenges inherent in the aging process.

Denial and avoidance don't serve us if we're sincerely interested in spiritual awakening. Take a slow, deep breath or two, and let your thoughts and feelings settle for a moment, the way snowflakes float to the ground inside a snow globe when you stop shaking it. Now notice what happens when you hear me say . . . one of the primary determinants of our happiness or suffering is the way we relate to change. This fundamental truth shows up in many of the perennial wisdom teachings. What we call 'aging' is essentially an increased awareness of changes that are taking place on the physical, mental, emotional, and spiritual levels of our lives. We can choose to see these changes as unfortunate problems, hassles, and tragedies, as many of us do much of the time. We can also choose to see them as a spiritual *curriculum* for discovering our true nature in the second half of life. When we make the latter choice, we begin to realize just how important it is to have a wise view of our human predicament. We come to see that our whole life is our practice. What the Taoist teachings call 'the ten thousand joys and the ten thousand sorrows' are all included. Our task, if we choose to accept it, is to manifest presence, wisdom, and lovingkindness as we endlessly deepen our understanding of the timeless mystery that we each ultimately embody."

As we saw in the previous chapter on committing to inner work, the act of living (which includes the various changes we associate with aging) involves an ongoing stream of encounters with our own physical sensations, emotions, and thoughts. These can give rise to profound meaning and can be quite intense at times, which leads us directly into our exploration of the fifth key to aging wisely and loving well. I call it "effective suffering."

I first heard this phrase from meditation teacher Shinzen Young, who used it in a story he told about the renowned Christian contemplative Thomas Merton.[1] Merton lived quite a bohemian life before he converted to Catholicism and then entered one of the church's strictest and most ascetic monastic orders. When he was asked about his decision and the suffering that such a lifestyle involved, Merton said that he didn't become a Trappist monk so he would suffer more than other people but that he wanted to learn to suffer more effectively.

I found the idea of effective suffering quite off-putting at first. *Who in the world wants to suffer?* I asked myself. *Let alone effectively, whatever that means.* When I looked deeply at the phrase and spent time reflecting on it, however, I recalled a number of similar teachings I'd heard from other teachers I respect. The epigraph at the beginning of this chapter—Ajahn Chah's helpful delineation between the two kinds of suffering—is one example. Another is something Ram Dass used to say often, that "despair is the necessary prerequisite for the next level of consciousness." His teacher, Neem Karoli Baba, gave similar teachings. "Suffering is grace," he was known to say. "Suffering brings me

closer to God." And from the influential Zen teacher Charlotte Joko Beck: "As you embrace the suffering of life, the
wonder shows up. They go together."[2]

I think it's safe to say that no living being, human or non-
human, wants to suffer. I also think it's safe to say that every
human being (and I imagine every sentient being) suffers
at times. There seems to be no getting around the fact that
embodied life involves difficulties on a variety of levels.
This is what the Buddha pointed out in the first of his four
noble truths: life involves suffering.

As obvious as this fact seems to me now, I can look back
on earlier parts of my life and see that I didn't really believe
it to be true. Other people often looked happier than I felt.
Perhaps they were simply better actors, or perhaps they
really were healthier, more joyful people. Lost as I was in
unconscious mental and emotional patterns that perpet-
uated the disharmony in my inner world, I interpreted the
suffering in my life as "my problem." I wrestled with deep
feelings of inadequacy and told myself stories in which I
was somehow to blame for my unhappiness. It was only
years later, when I studied Eastern and Western psychology,
that I came to understand how few people come through
childhood without their version of similar feelings to my
own. As the author Mary Karr put it, "A dysfunctional family
is any family with more than one person in it."[3]

When I was twenty-four, shortly after moving to Boulder, Colorado, to attend the inaugural summer program
at Naropa Institute (now Naropa University), a friend suggested I see an astrologer to get some guidance for the next

steps in my life. While the astrology reading was not a life-changer, the astrologer and I had a very powerful connection and soon became romantically involved. Our first three months together were an ascent unlike any I had experienced before in an intimate relationship. The phrase "falling in love" took on a new and truly magical meaning in my life. Within weeks, I moved into her house, connected deeply with her toddler, and convinced myself that my life was *finally* coming together. Sadly, the conventional wisdom that what goes up must come down proved to be the case, and shortly before the holiday season, we parted ways. The emotional descent was brutal, and our breakup left my heart feeling shattered into a thousand pieces.

I quickly concocted a story in which this "failed relationship" was simply more evidence that I was too wounded a human being to ever find and sustain a committed intimate partnership. That's when a close friend of mine gave me a holiday gift, a copy of *Cutting Through Spiritual Materialism* by the Buddhist teacher Chögyam Trungpa. Because I felt so raw and open, I was able to take in what the book was saying in a way that felt deeply transformative. Specifically, I understood what he was saying about the first noble truth. He made the point repeatedly that unsatisfactoriness is an existential given in a human life. The process of awakening, from a spiritual perspective, begins and continues with the acceptance of this unsettling fact.

For many of us, suffering of one kind or another is what motivates us to explore spiritual teachings in the first place. Yes, it's true that there are people who step onto the path because they have a passionate intellectual curiosity about "how it all is" and "what's really going on." Others seem to have a karmic jump-start at an early age that enables them to see through the superficial aspects of modern life and focus on its deepest meaning. Still, my experience is that the vast majority of people who see themselves as being on a spiritual journey are motivated to awaken by a desire to move beyond their personal suffering. I believe it's for this reason that Ajahn Chah, Thomas Merton, and many other teachers regularly made comments like those previously mentioned. They invite us to choose to see our painful experiences as what Ram Dass would call "grist for the mill of awakening."

What, then, is the next step after fully acknowledging the truth of suffering? How can we really learn to make our suffering more effective in relation to our spiritual maturation? It's very tempting to simply yield to our deep-seated conditioning to avoid suffering at all costs. If we give up our sense of agency and autonomy in this way, we become "driven to distraction," giving ourselves over to the always available options for turning away from what's happening in the present moment. In doing so, we undermine our amazing capacity to awaken to reality as it actually is, to embody and express the profound truth of our own essential nature.

A different option is to *intentionally move toward* the challenges and difficulties in our lives. This seems counterintuitive at first, because it goes against so many of our personal, social, and biological instincts. Indeed, even longtime, highly realized practitioners find themselves turning away from suffering before they know they're doing it and needing to remind themselves, through practice, to turn back toward it. Rachel Naomi Remen, an author, physician, and teacher of integrative medicine, described her understanding of this process in her book *Kitchen Table Wisdom*:

> Those who don't love themselves as they are rarely love life as it is either. Most people have come to prefer certain of life's experiences and deny and reject others, unaware of the value of the hidden things that may come wrapped in plain or even ugly paper. In avoiding all pain and seeking comfort at all costs, we may be left without intimacy or compassion; in rejecting change and risk we often cheat ourselves of the quest; in denying our suffering we may never know our strength or our greatness. Or even that the love we have been given can be trusted.
>
> It is natural, even instinctive to prefer comfort to pain, the familiar to the unknown. But sometimes our instincts are not wise. Life usually offers us far more than our biases and preferences will allow us to have. Beyond comfort lie grace, mystery, and adventure. We may need to let go of our beliefs and ideas about life in order to have life.
>
> The loss of an emotional or spiritual integrity may be at the source of our suffering. In a very paradoxical way, pain may point the way toward a

greater wholeness and become a potent force in the healing of this suffering.[4]

As we become increasingly able to be with our suffering rather than push away from it, we naturally develop a certain kind of curiosity about it. We become like researchers who adjust their microscope from 10× magnification to 50× to get a better look. Perhaps we sense that understanding suffering will be a key to moving beyond it. When we examine suffering in this way, we see that it's like a jewel with many facets. We realize that there are different kinds of suffering and that the way we work with suffering depends on what kind we're experiencing.

I've found it very helpful to make a distinction between what I call "existential suffering" and "unnecessary suffering." The first type is related to the human condition. We're all born, and we all have physical bodies. We all age with the passing of time and become ill at points along the way. All of us will die when our time comes. We will all be separated from those we love and from the things we care about most. We all live in a world that is constantly changing on every conceivable level, from the subatomic to the intergalactic. We all experience a seemingly endless stream of physical sensations, emotional states, sense contacts, and thoughts over which we have little or no control. We all have parts of ourselves that seek security and safety in a world that cannot reliably offer either one. I think of these facts as existential givens that apply to all human beings.

What varies a great deal from one person to the next is the

way we *respond* to these unavoidable realities. This is where the world's wisdom teachings can help us. If we're willing to learn, they will show us how to meet our moments of suffering with self-compassion and wisdom. They will teach us to see how our moments of suffering can give rise to insights that deepen our compassion for others who are suffering. They will allow us to glimpse the possibility of true freedom, to merge into the part of our being that bears witness to our common humanity while also residing in the ever-present equanimity of the Eternal Now. In other words, they will teach us the deep meaning of the phrase "effective suffering."

Buddhist tradition offers us a set of reflections, "objects of contemplation," that remind us of these fundamental truths. In some monastic traditions, these recollections are recited as part of the daily liturgy. Their effect is subtle yet powerful. When I worked with them for an extended period of time as a prelude to my morning meditation practice, I found that they energized my practice and exposed deeply held societal beliefs I had taken in without even knowing it. On some level, I believed that I was invulnerable, that "shit happens" didn't apply to me. More importantly, I believed that I wasn't going to die, at least not for a very long time. Of course, I intellectually understood the inevitability of death, as most of us do. Still, I didn't really live my life as if I believed it to be true. How astounding that I could live in a world filled with people who are dying day in and day out and persist in believing it wasn't going to happen to me!

I encourage you to explore these reflections for yourself.

To do so, sit quietly for a few moments, close your eyes or look down slightly with a soft focus, and notice the rhythm of your breath as you allow it to come and go of its own accord. Gently release any tendency to control or manipulate the breath. When you feel as if the busyness has settled somewhat in your mind-stream, read the following statements, preferably aloud, pausing for a time after each one. Be open to whatever you notice, understanding that there's no "correct" response.

FIVE DAILY RECOLLECTIONS

1. I am of the nature to grow old; I cannot avoid aging.
2. I am subject to illness and infirmity; I cannot avoid illness and infirmity.
3. I am of the nature to die; I cannot avoid death.
4. I will be parted from all that is dear and beloved to me.
5. I am the owner of my actions and heir to my actions. Actions are the womb from which I have sprung. My actions are my relations; my actions are my protection. The fruits of all my action, both wholesome and unwholesome, skillful and unskillful, I will inherit.[5]

At first glance, this practice often generates aversion and contributes to the common misunderstanding that Buddhist teachings are grim and nihilistic. Nothing could be further from the truth. This teaching is simply reminding us of what's true. Facing reality can be a great source of inspiration that enables us to appreciate each moment, to recognize our attachments, and to willingly exit our comfort zone. Only then can we wholeheartedly surrender to our deep yearning to awaken as completely as possible in whatever precious time we have on this earth. Put another way, these recollections expose and cut through our self-deceptions and clarify our true priorities.

That being said, I would caution that this particular practice is not appropriate for every individual, at least not at certain times. It's wise to work with it if it challenges you in a useful way, which sometimes will involve mild to moderate feelings of anxiety, sadness, or grief. On the other hand, if you are experiencing acute grief, are in clinical treatment for anxiety or depression, or struggle a lot with those moods and emotional states, you may find that these reflections increase distress in an unhelpful way. If that is your experience, consult with a qualified meditation teacher or a mental health professional who has a transpersonal perspective on their work. This practice is one of *many* tools we can use to liberate ourselves from unskillful habits of mind that create suffering for ourselves and others. There are many more to choose from, and one aspect of cultivating wisdom is learning to make appropriate choices about which methods to use at a given point in time.

One of the great joys of teaching conscious aging programs in a variety of places throughout the United States as well as in Canada and Ireland has been meeting people in the second half of their lives who have deeply integrated the principles of effective suffering. These people obliterate the negative stereotypes of aging that so many of us unconsciously embrace. Although they often don't know it, they serve as mentors to me, making it clear that elderhood can be an incredibly rich time of fruition and celebration rather than an irreversible descent into increasing irrelevance, loneliness, despair, and physical discomfort. These workshop participants seem to find their own unique ways to distinguish what I've called existential suffering and unnecessary suffering. They demonstrate a remarkable ability to accept aspects of their lives they have little or no control over and to reduce or eliminate responses that add extra suffering to already difficult situations.

One skill I've observed in many of these people is a psychological technique called "cognitive reframing," although many of them wouldn't have thought of what they were doing as a technique. Both Western psychology and Eastern teachings emphasize the role that our own perception plays in determining what we experience. Actress Shelley Winters offered an example of this process:

> I think on-stage nudity is disgusting, shameful, and damaging to all things American. But if I were 22 with a great body, it would be artistic, tasteful, patriotic, and a progressive religious experience.[6]

While this is obviously a light-hearted illustration, it clearly makes the point. She's showing us that the same phenomenon can be experienced in different ways depending on our viewpoint. For those of us who aspire to live awakened lives, this particular skill has far-reaching implications. We've already acknowledged the negative age-related beliefs, and their life-denying effects, that are common in our culture. What happens when we bring the skill of reframing to the realities of advanced old age? In his essay "Growing Old," the writer Aleksandr Solzhenitsyn gives a view of aging with an entirely different flavor than the views we commonly come across in modern Western society:

> How much easier it is then, how much more receptive we are to death, when advancing years guide us softly to our end. Aging thus is in no sense a punishment from on high but brings us its own blessings and a warmth of colors all its own. . . . There is even warmth to be drawn from the waning of your own strength compared to the past—just to think how sturdy I once used to be! You can no longer get through a whole day's work at one stretch, but how good it is to slip into the brief oblivion of sleep, and what a gift to wake once more to the clarity of your second or third morning of the day. And your spirit can find delight in limiting your intake of food, in abandoning the pursuit of novel flavors. You are still of this life, yet you are rising above the material

plane. . . . Growing old serenely is not a downhill path but an ascent.[7]

When I first read what Solzhenitsyn had to say, I felt a great sense of delight. The feeling was similar to the one I had when I met Reb Zalman and realized how completely he embraced his elderhood. It's not that he and Solzhenitsyn didn't suffer from the infirmities of old age. It's quite likely that Solzhenitsyn was living with many of the challenges associated with being a frail elder. The friend who sent me his quote told me the great writer was almost ninety when he wrote those words. I worked closely with Reb Zalman for a number of years, and I know that he had some difficult health problems. Still, they both learned how to turn poison into medicine, how to appreciate the lives they had and the growth potential in their hardships. I believe we are all capable of learning the same life lessons as these inspiring exemplars.

EFFECTIVE SUFFERING IN THE FACE OF DEATH

I've heard it said that our own death is what each of us ultimately fears most. Perhaps that's why our culture has developed so many different ways to avoid facing this most mysterious and unavoidable reality. If it's really true that *our life is our practice*, then even the experience of facing death could be something we're able to turn toward and recognize as part of the curriculum of conscious living. This often involves opening to physical pain, feelings of loss, and difficult questions like, "Did I live the life I most deeply wanted to live?"

I got to know David Mendosa when he wandered into a weekly meditation group I was teaching in a rented fellowship hall at the Unitarian Universalist Church of Boulder. An active church member, he'd seen a flyer about our sangha (practice community) on a church bulletin board and was curious about what we were doing. He felt immediately at home, started attending our weekly meetings, and became a member of our service committee (a group of volunteers who handle the many logistical tasks required to operate our small nonprofit organization).

Twelve years later, at the age of eighty-one, David had significantly deepened his meditation practice and become a committed environmental activist. He had sold his car and relied on friends and public transportation to move about. He made a point of attending an annual weeklong retreat I taught every summer at Shambhala Mountain Center in the mountains near Fort Collins, Colorado. I usually helped him find a ride to and from the retreat. He had called me in March 2017 to ask for assistance, and I had contacted some Boulder retreatants who offered to provide his transportation. I sent him an e-mail to let him know we had his rides handled.

He e-mailed me back and, to my surprise, told me his situation had changed, and he would no longer be attending the retreat:

Thank you, David. But my plans have changed. The reason I missed the sangha on Tuesday evening was because I went to a hospital Tuesday morning. A CT scan that morning indicated that I have liver cancer. They then biopsied my liver and I got the results yesterday afternoon. This cancer, a rare type called angiosarcoma of the liver, is incurable. The prognosis is poor but I haven't seen an oncologist yet to see what my alternatives are (surgery is out because it has already so thoroughly invaded the liver).

The pain is manageable with morphine pills around the clock. Of course, the diagnosis on Tuesday was a complete surprise but somehow I was completely prepared for it, and my mood has been completely positive since then—partly because I immediately dropped my most burdensome obligations.

In respect to your offering to help me get a ride to your retreat at the Shambhala Mountain Center, I don't expect to still be around when the retreat comes. So that's one less obligation for you.

Be well, David[8]

David died at home about a month after his diagnosis. I spoke with him a couple of times after I received his e-mail, and we had warm, heartfelt conversations. Other sangha members visited with him as well and reported that he maintained his positive outlook and sense of feeling completely prepared right to the end. I felt a deep sadness when I learned of his death, even though I knew it was coming. At the same time, I felt hopeful and energized in relation to my own journey because I had just witnessed the fruit of committed spiritual practice.

What comes to mind now when I remember David is a Zen teaching I learned at Upaya Zen Center when I was part of a teaching team there in 2009. At the end of our practice day, we would finish the last meditation period, and Roshi Joan Halifax would lead us in a recitation that we all spoke in unison:

Life and death are of supreme importance.
Time passes swiftly and opportunity is lost.
Let us Awaken! Awaken!
Do not squander your life.

What is it I'm really trying to say in this chapter and the preceding one? Those of us who aspire to awaken spiritually have access to time-tested practices and principles that have been used for millennia to bring our best human qualities to fruition. We start by opening to what life presents, however mysterious or unexpected that may be. We train ourselves to turn toward whatever arises, be it pleasant, unpleasant, or neutral. We then cultivate loving curiosity, a blend of self-compassion and a spirit of investigation. Recognizing the remarkable number of skillful methods and perspectives that are available to us, we explore creative ways to open our hearts, quiet our minds, and become instruments of love and wisdom in the world. The last part of the process is to pause periodically to reflect on our unfolding journey and to remember yet again that we already *have* what we seek and we already *are* what we yearn to become.

CHAPTER SIX
SERVING FROM THE HEART

I slept and dreamt that life was joy.

I awoke and saw that life was service.

I acted and behold, service was joy.

—Rabindranath Tagore

WHEN I WAS the education and training director of the Spiritual Eldering Institute, I led many workshops for people who wanted to live fully and love well in the second half of their lives. I often used a goal-setting exercise to help them develop a clear picture of their next steps on the journey of awakening. In my work as a spiritual counselor and life coach, I've given the same assignment to many individuals. Almost everyone who worked with the exercise wrote about wanting to "make a contribution," to leave the world a better place than it was when they arrived in it. I refer to this aspiration—the sixth of our keys in this book—as "serving from the heart," and I have seen it in every approach to spiritual maturation I've come across. Even when it starts out as a "should," as it often does, service work catalyzes the seeker's evolution from a frequently self-absorbed individual to an increasingly selfless instrument of the Great Way, the Divine, the Tao.

In the last chapter we explored the ways in which effective suffering contributes to this natural unfolding. It enables us to recognize the functional and necessary role that our difficulties play in deepening our realization of the two truths—the relative and the absolute. In the early stages of conscious service work, there is typically a significant amount of ego involvement and attachment to results. Our underlying ego-needs for approval and validation loom large and are repeatedly exposed, both to ourselves and to others. Painful and disconcerting as this process may be, it gradually teaches us to "disidentify" with being the "doer" of our actions. Instead, we come to see that "helping out" is an organic expression of our deepest nature and that we are simply playing our unique part in the overall scheme of things.

Intuitive wisdom helps us to recognize and claim our gifts, to acknowledge our weaknesses, and to be mindful of our stage of life and the specifics of our living situation. This information feeds into our inner guidance, the aspect of our being that Ajahn Chah called "the one who knows." We learn to attune to whatever forms of service life calls us to perform at a given point in time. This commitment to serving from the heart takes us through a wide range of joys and sorrows that deepen our understanding of compassion in action. The more we serve others in this way, the more we come to embody loving awareness and gain insight into the nondual nature of ultimate reality.

The basic inclination to care about one another and to serve those in need, to be what the Dalai Lama calls "a force for good," is part of our evolutionary inheritance as human beings. Ryokan, a beloved poet in the Zen tradition, expressed his heart's desire in a simple yet powerful way that speaks to our hearts, too:

> O, that my priest's robe were wide enough
> to gather up all the suffering people
> In this floating world.[1]

At the initial meeting of the Seva Foundation, a public health organization I worked with in Nepal from 1987 to 1990, this perspective was expressed poetically in a kind of commitment ceremony:

> Clear cold light of winter sun through leafless trees
>   by a frozen lake
> People meeting there for a common purpose
>   People from different places
>   leading different lives
> Doctors and bureaucrats, wisemen and
>   professional madmen, tree farmers and students
>   who shared only one thing in common
> A desire so great as to be a need

the need to serve
　　to do something to relieve human suffering.
We are not here to wait for the perfect society
　　since we are not perfect ourselves.
Nor have we the obsessive belief
　　that we can make all beings happy.
We have, however, the certitude
　　that much of the world's suffering
　　is unfair and avoidable.
And we pledge ourselves to do something about it
　　by this lake in December,
　　surrounded by oak trees, leafless yet
　　waiting confidently for spring . . .
　　we pledge ourselves to serve.[2]

Having worked with a variety of nonprofit organizations and schools, I've come to see this service ethic in a wide range of people. I deeply honor and appreciate our innate desire to be of benefit to others. I see this yearning as being rooted in our recognition that we're all part of an interdependent web in which the healing of any one part supports the healing of the whole. Children, when behaving at their best, express this deeply embedded knowing through acts of kindness and generosity. Those among us who have suffered most deeply are sometimes blessed with extraordinary empathy that gives rise to spontaneous compassion in a way that inspires all of us. The following story illustrates what I mean:

A few years ago at the Seattle Special Olympics, nine contestants, all physically or mentally disabled, assembled at the starting line for the 100-yard dash. At the gun they all started out, not exactly in a dash, but with the relish to run the race to the finish and win.

All, that is, except one boy who stumbled on the asphalt, tumbled over a couple of times, and began to cry. The other eight heard the boy cry. They slowed down and paused. Then they all turned around and went back. Every one of them. One girl with Down's syndrome bent down and kissed him and said, "This will make it better." Then all nine linked arms and walked together to the finish line.

Everyone in the stadium stood, and the cheering went on for 10 minutes.[3]

Given the reality of our basic goodness and the evidence we see around us that supports its existence, many of us struggle with the question of why there is so much human-caused, unnecessary suffering on our beautiful blue-green planet. We human beings have the potential to be incredibly wise and deeply loving, and we also have deep-seated tendencies to be aggressive, greedy, and deluded. Thich Nhat Hanh likened these evolutionary patterns that exist in all of us to seeds embedded in our consciousness. He taught that whichever seeds we water with our habits of body, speech, and mind will be the ones that grow, while the opposite seeds will atrophy. This same understanding is echoed in a story from the Native American tradition:

> A grandmother is teaching her granddaughter about life. She says, "A fight is going on inside me. It's a terrible fight between two wolves. One wolf is angry, envious, regretful, despairing, greedy, arrogant, self-pitying, guilty, resentful, and lies. The other wolf is joyful, peaceful, loving, hopeful, serene, humble, grateful, kind, generous, compassionate, truthful, and full of faith. The same fight is going on inside of you and every other human being, too.
>
> The granddaughter thinks about this and asks her grandmother, "Which wolf will win?"
>
> The old grandmother says simply, "The one you feed."[4]

To the extent that our contemplative practices and our service activities reinforce our sense of superiority, specialness, or uniqueness, we feed the wolf who perpetuates suffering in our own lives and in the world, oftentimes unknowingly. To the extent that we purify our intentions and surrender our ego-agendas, we become true instruments of healing, blessing, and liberation that spread love, compassion, and well-being in whatever we do. Even when things don't go according to plan, which is often the case, we can turn straw into gold by forgiving ourselves for our unskillfulness and committing ourselves to learning from our mistakes.

There's a Zen saying attributed to Dōgen Zenji, the founder of the Sōtō school of Japanese Zen: "Life is one continuous mistake."[5] Because I believe that my entire life is inseparable from my "practice," I've chosen to modify that comment into a statement that better supports my awakening and the awakening of people I work with, many of whom identify themselves as spiritual practitioners: *The entire spiritual path is one continuous mistake.* I find great comfort in those words because they undermine my deeply conditioned tendency to be a perfectionist, to have unrealistically high expectations of myself and others. Little by little, I've come to understand the last letter I read in a delightful book called *Children's Letters to God*. It said, "Dear God, I'm doing the best I can. Frank."[6]

A key issue that often arises in helping others involves motivation. Buddhist psychology teaches that every voluntary action is preceded by an intention. While this may be a subtle process on one level, it's a critically important aspect of serving from the heart. Mindfulness training enables us to become aware of our intentions, and that awareness, in turn, allows us to notice which part of our being is expressing itself. Am I helping because I want to be liked or admired, perceived as a "good person"? To feel useful? To alleviate guilt? To feel powerful? To avoid feeling the pain being triggered by someone else's suffering? Or am I reaching out because I see clearly what needs to be done and that I'm the appropriate person to do it? Is my effort to alleviate suffering rooted in an internal "should" of some kind? Or could the act of service be likened to the right hand assisting the left, both hands clearly recognizing they are part of the same cosmic body?

I don't want to romanticize the challenges associated with questions like these. Most of them don't have simple answers. Our motives for helping often derive from a blend of our own needs and the heartfelt compassion of our true nature. Understanding this dynamic is one of the central tasks on the path of service and inspires us to ask ourselves who it is we think is being of service. How inspiring it is to see people who show the forbearance to avoid superficial responses and instead *live* their way into the answers.

Books and teachings can support us in discovering what moves us to help out. Over time, we come to see that our conceptual models of effective service evolve into what I call "practice wisdom," an integrated way of being with others that includes book knowledge and goes beyond it to an experience of *deep knowing*—which, ironically, includes its opposite, *not knowing*. This paradox is highlighted in many of the world's wisdom traditions.

Consider the following example. In the late 1970s and early 1980s, I was fascinated with the kind of personal growth work that is done in groups. I was teaching Gestalt therapy and leading several personal growth groups a week. The groups had a wildness and unpredictability about them, qualities that often pushed both the participants and me beyond our comfort zones into places that were exciting, vulnerable, and fully authentic. I often felt like I was privileged to be seeing people when they were being as real as human beings could ever be.

In one meeting, we did an opening check-in, and everyone took a few minutes to update the group on their experiences of the past week. Julie, a woman in her mid-thirties, was the last person to speak that day. She was normally extroverted and quick-witted; today, however, she seemed shy and withdrawn, almost whispering what she was saying so that I could hardly hear her. I leaned in and concentrated on both her words and her nonverbal communication. Her shoulders were rounded, she slumped forward a bit, and her lower lip was trembling ever so slightly.

"I just can't believe it," she said. "I just can't believe it."

"Can't believe what?" asked Rick, a group member sitting next to her.

"It's over . . . Rob called off our engagement," she said. "We sat down to plan our wedding for this summer, and he didn't seem into it at all. I asked him what was going on, and he became very quiet and looked away from me. Then he said he didn't want to get married. He said he'd been thinking about it for the last few months, and he realized that it wasn't the right thing, that he wanted to remain friends, but he didn't want to be romantically involved anymore."

At that point, Julie began to cry. At first she wept quietly, tears streaming down her cheeks. Then the dam broke and she began to sob, to let herself feel the deep grief and huge disappointment of her loss. It was excruciatingly painful to witness. The room became very still, and almost everyone in the group opened their hearts to silently create a space of compassionate refuge for Julie. There was one person, however, who was unable to maintain the silent, caring environment the group was creating.

Allison, who was sitting on a meditation cushion across the room, stood up and started walking toward Julie. I intervened immediately and said, "Stop, Allison. What's happening for you right now?"

"I can't just sit here like the rest of you. Can't you see Julie needs a hug and some comfort? Don't any of you *care* about what she's feeling?"

"Please go back to your seat and sit down," I said.

She remained standing for a few moments and looked at me with anger in her eyes. Then she returned to her seat and joined the rest of the group in giving Julie their healing attention and support.

Perhaps you've already guessed what was going on. All of us in the room that day except Allison understood that Julie feeling her grief was a necessary step in her healing process. When I later met with Allison individually to talk about the incident in the group, she told me that the previous year her own fiancé, Richard, had called off their wedding the day before it was to take place. I could see from the tears in her eyes that her feelings about her own loss were still painfully raw, and I helped Allison to understand that she'd been unable to tolerate the emotions triggered in her own heart by what Julie was sharing with the group.

Unaware of her unconscious agenda when she stood up in the group, Allison had perceived me as a heartless and unskillful psychotherapist. She had convinced herself that she was the only person in the room who had the courage to reach out when Julie was in need. Near the end of our debriefing meeting, Allison and I talked about her own need to mourn and heal. "When I feel brave enough, I'd like to follow in Julie's footsteps," she said. "Maybe at one of our sessions coming up."

This experience was one of many that helped me to see that good intentions, by themselves, are not enough to alleviate suffering. To borrow a phrase from mathematics, wholesome motivation in service work is "necessary but not sufficient." I didn't doubt for a moment that Allison was trying to be helpful. She really believed she was being compassionate and that she could assuage Julie's pain. What was missing was what Buddhist teachings call skillful means, a wise understanding of what was actually happening and a related repertoire of creative behaviors that could provide true healing and lasting benefit. It was clear to me that Julie needed a good cry and ongoing permission to mourn the loss of her intimate relationship with Rob. That's what would eventually allow her to accept what was happening and to move forward in her life with a sense of new possibilities.

THREE QUALITIES OF SKILLFUL SERVICE

What are some of the qualities and skills that enable us to serve effectively, with open hearts, quiet minds, and the courage to share our own vulnerability? While the list could be long, as is the case with the ten *paramis*—the Buddhist "perfections" discussed in the Theravada tradition—I would like to emphasize the importance of three particular qualities and the skills associated with each: presence, compassion, and humor.

Presence

The first of these, the quality of presence, involves being grounded in the here and now, and understanding that the present moment is always our fundamental reference point for reality. I remember Jack Kornfield speaking about this quality many years ago in a talk he gave. He described an experience he'd had when he was in Las Vegas. In the entry-way to one of the casinos, there was a sign he saw that said, "You Have to Be Present to Win." It turns out that this is true in every aspect of our lives and not just when we're out for an evening in Las Vegas.

One skill associated with presence is what I call "clear see-ing." This enables us to perceive what's actually happening in a situation, whether it's an internal emotional struggle, a one-to-one conversation, or a larger event of some kind. Because on one level we're resting in Being itself, which is timeless and still, we can respond appropriately rather than in a reactive, knee-jerk manner. We're able to see our own judging mind when it's triggered and to stand far enough behind it to see what's happening with a wise perspective.

In some cases, clear seeing involves a life-changing taste of self-transcendence. Consider the experience of the writer Elizabeth Herron.

I was depressed. The world had gone flat and col-
orless. I had withdrawn. I was a tiny kernel inside
my body, adrift amid necessities and obligations,
oppressed by my separateness, cut off from the
wellsprings of my soul. I walked up to the pond,
took off my clothes and plunged into the water—a
sudden shock, cold against my skin. Floating to
the surface, I heard a bird call across the meadow.
Suddenly, I was at the still point. The bird's call
was my voice. We were separate and yet one. I was
out there and in here. . . . All things converged in
me and radiated from me. "The center of the circle is everywhere; the circumference is nowhere."
I recognized this, knowing it had always been so,
though I had been cut off from my experience of it.
My head filled with poetic images. The dimension
of the infinite was everywhere.[7]

Realizing that we're each part of the same timeless mystery, separate yet one, "out there and in here," naturally
gives rise to a feeling of compassion. We feel moved to
serve from the heart. Why would we want to do anything
but help out if, even for one moment, we've been separated
from our separateness and merged into the unity behind
the diversity?

This heartfelt spaciousness balanced with sensitivity is
extremely beneficial when dealing with suffering of any
kind. It's not that we force ourselves into a calm, equan-
imous state because we're aversive to strong emotions.

It's more that the strong emotions are like isolated storm clouds in a boundless, blue sky that extends infinitely in every direction. Relative to the limitless space of the sky, the clouds seem small and workable, even when they're dark and ominous. Like the view from the summit of a high mountain, this aerial vision allows us to see the interrelationships of all the elements in the circumstance with which we're presented.

There are some other terms I use to talk about presence as well. They have different nuances, yet they all point in the same direction. One is *wakefulness*. Another is *aliveness*. I don't think it's an accident that the fruition of spiritual life is referred to as "waking up." When we are grounded in our physical bodies, connected to the earth in a palpable way, and in clear touch with the immediacy of our senses and emotions, we naturally experience what Eckhart Tolle calls "the power of now." We're able to function fully and to express the wisest, most loving aspects of our nature.

An additional skill that becomes accessible when we're not preoccupied with our ego-identity and have surrendered to the flow of Being that is our true nature is what Thich Nhat Hanh calls "deep listening." This innate capacity that we all share beautifully illustrates the complementarity of inner practices like meditation and compassionate action in the world.

Meditation and prayer teach us to listen inwardly to our bodies, our hearts, and our minds. As weeks of regular practice turn into months, years, and decades, we attune to these fields of awareness with increasing accuracy. We gradually brighten the light of our concentration and realize that we can direct it by aiming our attention at whatever we choose. When our choice is to attend to a person or other living being we care about and wish to benefit, the recipient feels the radiance of our awareness and responds as if being bathed in life-giving sunlight. Another word for this kind of attention is *love*.

The poet Mark Nepo captures this kind of open, wakeful listening in words that I revisit on a regular basis:

> To listen is to continually give up all expectation and to give our attention, completely and freshly, to what is before us, not really knowing what we will hear or what it will mean. In the practice of our days, to listen is to lean in, softly, with a willingness to be changed by what we hear.[8]

Sometimes feeling heard in this way is all we really need. In 1971, I went on a ten-day yoga retreat for the first time. I felt very inspired by Swami Satchidananda, the teacher who led the retreat, and I hung on his words in a way that reflected a much higher level of interest than I felt for the undergraduate college classes I was taking at the time. During one question-and-answer period, a middle-aged man sitting near me asked Swamiji if he did any kind of psychotherapy with people. His answer was one that I sometimes think about when I walk in the mountains of Colorado with a family member or close friend. He said, "When someone who is feeling troubled comes to see me,

I invite them to go for a walk in a place that is beautiful, perhaps around a lake or through the woods or in the hills. I ask them what is troubling them and then I really *listen*. They see the trees swaying in the breeze, the clouds floating by, the sun coming and going, perhaps they hear the water washing up on the shore. I keep listening. When we return, they feel better."

I had a personal experience of this kind in 1987, shortly after I first arrived in Nepal for an open-ended period of time. I had a number of reasons for being there, one of which was to attend the inaugural Namo Buddha Seminar. This was an opportunity to study and practice intensively with the Venerable Thrangu Rinpoche, a highly respected scholar and practitioner in the Tibetan Buddhist tradition, who was teaching Westerners for the first time. From the first dharma talk I heard him give, I was deeply moved by this gentle, warm, and erudite teacher. After the first two classes he taught, I spoke to his assistant and arranged a one-on-one meeting with Rinpoche.

I remember feeling nervous and excited as I walked up the front steps of his monastery near the Boudha Stupa in Kathmandu. I was aware that Rinpoche's ability to speak English was limited, though I'd been told that his passive vocabulary was actually pretty good. He looked at me with a soft, open expression, unhurried and fully present.

"Rinpoche," I said, "I'm here because I'd like to ask for your guidance in regard to my spiritual path. This is a time of great confusion, and while I have a deep wish to awaken,

I'm uncertain about which methods and practices are appropriate for me now."

"Tell me about your spiritual path," he said.

I responded with a ten-minute spiritual autobiography, starting with my upbringing. "I grew up in the Jewish tradition. I left Judaism when I was about fourteen. When I was in my early twenties, I began studying yoga and meditation, at first on my own, and then with Swami Satchidananda and Ram Dass. Then I met Isa, a Sufi teacher who came to Boulder to share the teachings of Hazrat Inayat Khan. Isa helped me to understand devotion in a new and deeper way. In 1975, I began training with Trungpa Rinpoche, who had opened Naropa Institute in Boulder, and I shifted my focus to Buddhist studies and practices. A couple of years later, I read Joseph Goldstein's book on insight meditation and decided to focus on vipassana practice as taught in the Theravada Buddhist tradition. In the early 1980s, I met Father Thomas Keating, a teacher of contemplative Christianity, who taught me what he called the Centering Prayer and shared his love of interspiritual dialogue."

I noticed that as I was telling Rinpoche my story, I felt an increasingly heavy feeling of shame and guilt. For years I'd been living with an intense inner critic that frequently harassed me: *You're digging too many shallow holes. Two years of this, three years of that, and four years of something else. You're as confused now as you were when you started all of this "awakening stuff" as a college student.*

After describing a few other teachings and traditions I'd

explored, the shame I felt was so burdensome that I had unconsciously rounded my shoulders, rolled forward on the meditation cushion, and lowered my face toward the ground. Just as I was about to finish what I was saying, I realized that I'd come to see Rinpoche to ask for yet *another* set of teachings. I was afraid to look up at him because I was certain he was simply going to point a finger toward the door and say, "Get out of here!"

When I peeked up at him, however, he was glowing with a broad smile. "Very good," he said. "Very good. All of these things are very good." He caught my eye to make sure I was taking in what he was saying. "I think anything that cultivates wisdom and compassion is very good." At that point, he spoke to me about a particular visualization practice he wanted me to do, and he said Phil, one of his senior Western students, would teach me the specifics of the technique.

I thanked him, put my palms together and bowed, then walked out into the hall. Until meeting with Rinpoche, I had been largely unaware of how much shame I'd been carrying for the past fifteen years. What crystallized the insight was my awareness of the complete absence of shame when I left our meeting, as if I had stopped carrying a heavy backpack I no longer needed. Even more amazing was the feeling I had when I was with Rinpoche that I was seeing myself through his eyes. On that level, he seemed to see only the purity of my desire to be liberated and to be an instrument of liberation in the world. All those years of self-judgment disappeared completely in one encounter with this highly realized teacher. I had read about what Tibetan teachings

call "transmission of mind," but I'd never quite understood
what that phrase meant. This felt like a glimpse of it.

Compassion

The second quality that enables us to be of true benefit
in the world is authentic compassion. This includes compassion for ourselves, compassion for other living beings,
and compassion for the earth. Like a Venn diagram, the
qualities of presence and compassion overlap in a way that
supports and strengthens our connection to our natural
good-heartedness.

For many of us, expressing compassion for others feels
easier than being kind to ourselves. Sometimes we see a
person with a problem, we know what to do, and we just do
it. Consider the example of Julio Diaz:

> Julio Diaz has a daily routine. Every night, the thirty-
> one-year-old social worker ends his hour-long sub-
> way commute to the Bronx one stop early, just so he
> can eat at his favorite diner.
>
> But one night last month, as Diaz stepped off
> the No. 6 train onto a nearly empty platform, his
> evening took an unexpected turn. He was walking
> toward the stairs when a teenage boy approached
> and pulled out a knife.
>
> "He wants my money, so I just gave him my wallet
> and told him, 'Here you go,'" says Diaz.
>
> As the teen began to walk away, Diaz told him,
> "Hey, wait a minute. You forgot something. If you're

going to be robbing people for the rest of the night, you might as well take my coat to keep you warm." The would-be robber looked at his would-be victim "like what's going on here?" Diaz says. "He asked me, 'Why are you doing this?'"

Diaz replied, "If you're willing to risk your freedom for a few dollars, then I guess you must really need money. I mean, all I wanted to do was get dinner, and if you really want to join me . . . hey, you're more than welcome.

"You know, I just felt maybe he really needed help," Diaz says.

He and the teen went into the diner and sat in a booth.

"The manager comes by, the dishwashers come by, the waiters come by to say hi," Diaz recalls. "The kid was like, 'You know everybody here. Do you own the place?'

"'No, I just eat here a lot,' I told him. He says, 'But you're even nice to the dishwasher.'"

Diaz replied, "Well, haven't you been taught you should be nice to everybody?"

"Yeah, but I didn't think people actually behaved that way," the teen said.

Diaz asked him what he wanted out of life. "He just had almost a sad face," Diaz says.

The teen couldn't answer Diaz—or he didn't want to.

When the bill arrived, Diaz told the teen, "Look, I

guess you're going to have to pay for this bill 'cause you have my money, and I can't pay for this. So if you give me my wallet back, I'll gladly treat you."

The teen "didn't even think about it" and returned the wallet, Diaz says. "I gave him twenty dollars. I figure maybe it'll help him. I don't know."

Diaz says he asked for something in return—the teen's knife—"and he gave it to me."

Afterward, when Diaz told his mother what had happened, she said, "You're the type of kid that if someone asked you for the time, you'd give them your watch."

"I figure, you know, if you treat people right, you can only hope that they treat you right. It's as simple as it gets in this complicated world."[9]

Self-compassion can best be understood as a skill. Because we've looked deeply at our own suffering and see it clearly, we've come to fully accept that some suffering is unavoidable. Rather than blame ourselves for our struggles and reinforce deep-seated feelings of unworthiness, we recognize that, in addition to the personal dimension of unhappiness, there's also an impersonal dimension. In other words, we come to see both the uniqueness and the universality of our difficulties. We finally resolve to surrender our perfectionism completely because we can see that it is rooted in delusion and undermines our appreciation for our personal lives and for life itself.

The writer Anne Lamott offers us a glimpse of how

self-compassion looks in someone who has cultivated it over an extended period of time:

> Sometimes faith looks like myopia: I don't see everyone's faults so clearly as I used to, let alone my own. The God of my later years is not interested in my pores, or cellulite, and hopes that I will stop noticing yours. My vision has blessedly blurred. This is a great advantage when you're trying to live more spiritually, more expansively, more like Zorba the Greek and less like the Church Lady. For instance, when I sit on my bed now writing on my iPad, the top roll of my tummy sometimes creeps over onto the screen and starts typing away. In the old days, upon noticing this unsought collaboration, I would have decided to start a new diet, or to end it all. Now I think, "Who knows? Maybe it's got something interesting to add."[10]

The essence of wise self-care is balance. We may have grown up in a situation where shame and guilt played a major role in our family life. Such feelings make it difficult to treat ourselves in a loving way and to feel deserving of nurturance. It's a rare individual who emerges from their family of origin experience without some unhealed wounds.

This understanding can be useful in teaching yourself to be your own best friend. I've often worked with people who beat themselves up relentlessly. One approach I use in these situations is to ask the person how they would respond to a loved one or close friend who was struggling with the same issue they are. Inevitably, their face softens, and they say something like, "I'd tell her to stop being so hard on herself." Or "I'd give him a gift certificate for a massage." Or "I'd tell them about a similar problem I had last year." We know what's needed much of the time, especially with people we're close to. The harshness of our inner dialogues and the high expectations we place on ourselves are what block access to what we know.

Healthy self-care is kind yet not indulgent. It's a gesture of self-love in the positive sense and not self-absorption in the narcissistic sense. We take care of our bodies, our hearts, and our minds because we understand that this life we've been given is a sacred gift. A strong, healthy body helps us to awaken, to experience joy, and to offer our gifts to the world. We don't deny that we'll eventually get sick, grow old, and die, and we're accepting of the fact that we often have little or no control over what will happen to us.

We simply do what we can to optimize our quality of life for our own benefit and, simultaneously, for the benefit of others. Rather than obsess about every seemingly imperfect situation that arises, we understand that such moments are inherent in the human condition, we allow them to be as they are, and we stop doing battle with reality. This allows us to rest in peace—while we're still alive. We can laugh at the well-known words, "Life is just one damn thing after another."

This self-compassion gives new meaning to the phrase

"My heart goes out to you." We become more empathetic, less judgmental, and truly appreciative of how vulnerable and poignant our daily lives feel when our hearts are open. Just as the yin-yang symbol of the Tao intertwines white and black colors, the joys and sorrows of our lives weave a seamless existential tapestry that teaches us to say yes to our lives again and again and again.

I stand by the bed where a young woman lies, her face postoperative, her mouth twisted in palsy, clownish. A tiny twig of the facial nerve, the one to the muscles of her mouth, has been severed. She will be thus from now on. As surgeon, I had followed with religious fervor the curve of her flesh, I promise you that. Nevertheless, to remove the tumor in her cheek, I had to cut the little nerve.

Her young husband is in the room. He stands on the opposite side of the bed, and together they seem to dwell in the evening lamplight, isolated from me, private. "Who are they," I ask myself, "he and this wry mouth who gaze and touch each other so generously?"

The woman speaks:

"Will my mouth always be like this?" she asks.

"Yes," I say. "It is because the nerve was cut."

She nods, is silent. But the young man smiles.

"I like it," he says. "It's kind of cute."

All at once I know who he is. I understand, and I lower my gaze. One is not bold in an encounter with a god. Unmindful of my presence, he bends to kiss her crooked mouth, and I'm so close I can see how he twists his own lips to accommodate hers, to show her that their kiss still works.

I remember that the gods appeared in ancient Greece as mortals, and I hold my breath and let the wonder in.[11]

Humor

The last quality I want to highlight in relation to serving from the heart is humor. While at first glance, humor and our efforts to relieve suffering may appear to be strange bedfellows, that's not the case at all. There's a particular type of humor that is rooted in lovingkindness rather than contempt, derision, or bitterness. Because we've cultivated presence in our lives and learned to be compassionate with ourselves and others, we can appreciate the ironies, absurdities, and enigmas that touch *every* human life at some point along the way. We come to recognize the value of playfulness and lightheartedness, which provide temporary relief from the intensity of the pain and sorrow. These bursts of emotional sunshine in our lives strengthen our resilience and remind us that we can still appreciate life even in the midst of hurt, loss, anger, and disappointment.

When I was a hospice director in New Mexico, we had a contest to rename the organization's newsletter. Some of the entries submitted by staff members were quite irreverent, so we created a spoof version of the contest alongside the actual contest. This reflected a backstage playfulness that energized us so we could continue our daily work with people who were often suffering greatly from advanced cancer and other end-stage illnesses. There was no disrespect intended, and we were consistently cautious to make sure we avoided hurting the feelings of patients and family members. One of my tasks as the director was to announce the winning entry to the staff members who had participated in the spoof version of the contest. First prize went to "The Last Breath," and the runner-up was "The Terminal News."

The same sense of what some Buddhists call "sad-joy" is evident in an e-mail I received in 2013 from a friend and mentor, James Baraz, one of the founders of Spirit Rock Meditation Center in California.[12]

> Dear Friends,
> I wanted to share with you that my mom, Selma Baraz, died Tuesday evening at 9:53pm.
>
> It was a peaceful and beautiful passing with my sister Susan, my older son, Tony, her attendant, Letty, and me by her side. For the previous few hours she had been completely unresponsive until just a few moments before she left. Then she opened her eyes and took in the love around her. We all told her we loved her and she tried to mouth something which we all agreed was conveying, "I love you, too." And then she was gone.

My mom was an amazing, unforgettable human being. As my sister put it: movie star stunning, she was a force of nature—smart as a whip, cutting, sharp NY sarcastic, ferocious defender of all those she loved, politically aware and astute, champion of AIDS causes (AIDS volunteer of the year), business woman extraordinaire at a time women weren't, book lover, cook beyond compare, theater goer, world traveler, brutal Scrabble player, who loved to give and put family above all.

Her humor was legendary. On that last day before I flew down to be at her side, I spoke to her by phone, knowing she could hardly speak. I said, "Mom, I just want you to know that I love you. I know it's hard to talk so please don't exert yourself." Barely able to get the words out, she whispered, "Now you tell me!" That was my mom.

I'll miss you, Mom. And I'm deeply grateful for all you've given me and the world in your 94 years.

I love you,
James

The key to using this kind of humor in a way that supports conscious service work is to be crystal clear about our motivation. If there's even a hint of passive aggression or one-upmanship toward another person, significant misunderstandings can arise. If our intention is genuinely compassionate, and we're speaking as much to ourselves as to others, this lightness of being can go a long way toward reminding us of the joy of service that Rabindranath Tagore wrote about in the epigraph to this chapter.

Pope Francis, the current head of the Catholic Church, offers us one last example of the way humor can support our awakening and our efforts to awaken others. Posted outside the door to his office is a sign that says, "Complaining is forbidden. Offenders are subject to a syndrome of victimhood that reduces their sense of humor and capacity to solve problems. For anyone caught whining in front of children, sanctions will be doubled. To become the best of yourself, you must focus on your own potential and not on your limits. So stop complaining and act to change your life for the better."[13]

I see this chapter as the "heart center" of this book. Perhaps that's because service work has played such a central role in my own life. Or perhaps because it plays such a central role in so many of the world's wisdom traditions. In any case, I want to review the key points I've addressed in this chapter and create a context for the chapter that follows.

Effective suffering, as discussed in chapter 5, plants a seed that inspires us to contribute to our collective well-being. Altruism is rooted in our evolutionary heritage. Motivation is a key, and it can be wholesome or unwholesome. We function best when we see ourselves as choice-makers who can gradually learn to serve selflessly from the heart. To optimize the benefits of our service activities, we need to cultivate specific qualities of our being, including presence, compassion, and a light touch in our work.

Albert Einstein sums up the essence of this chapter beautifully:

> A human being is part of the whole called by us "Universe," a part limited in time and space. He experiences himself, his thoughts and feelings, as something separated from the rest, a kind of *optical delusion of his consciousness.* This delusion is a kind of prison for us, restricting us to our personal desires and to affection for a few persons nearest to us. Our task must be to free ourselves from this prison by widening our circle of compassion to embrace all living creatures and the whole of nature in its beauty. Nobody is able to achieve this completely, but the striving for such achievement is in itself a part of the liberation and a foundation for inner security.[14]

CHAPTER SEVEN
CELEBRATING THE JOURNEY

These days I'm the advance scout for the experiences
of aging, and I've come back from the scouting party
to bring good news. The good news is that the spirit is
more powerful than the vicissitudes of aging.
—RAM DASS

THE DALAI LAMA attended a meeting of the Mind and Life
Institute, a group of scientists and spiritual practitioners
who gather periodically to discuss their common interest
in scientific and contemplative approaches to exploring
the nature of reality. Part of the meeting involved a distinguished Japanese researcher, a specialist in laughter,
sharing the results of a recent study. He concluded his
presentation, the last one of the day, by asking the Dalai
Lama a question: "Your Holiness, can you tell us what was
the happiest moment of your life?" The audience, which
included Buddhist scholars, meditation practitioners, scientists, and a hundred guests, became silent and very attentive. His Holiness paused for a time, reflected thoughtfully,

then suddenly said in a booming voice, "I think . . . now!" Everyone in the room laughed with delight, and the meeting was adjourned.[1]

Some natural questions that arise when we consider the process of spiritual development in the second half of life are: Do we ever truly "arrive"? How will we know when we do? Phrases like "spiritual path" and "journey of awakening" imply a movement of some kind, from one "place" to another, or perhaps more accurately, from one mode of being to another. The way I like to phrase this inquiry is "What are the fruits of a spiritually mature life?" We generally recognize them when we see them, and we're drawn to spend time with people who embody them. Who wouldn't want to be with someone for whom the happiest moment of their life is now? Yet we don't often identify and look deeply at our most excellent human qualities, all of which are desperately needed in today's world. What does it mean in our fast-paced, pluralistic, and secularized society to aspire to the qualities of wise elderhood?

It's clear to all of us, I imagine, that growing old does not in and of itself lead to wisdom and lovingkindness. We've probably all met elderly people who are angry, frightened, self-absorbed, or hard to communicate with. It's a safe assumption that they became the way they are because of pain, suffering, and confusion in their lives, and it's very important that we witness their unhappiness with compassion and not with judgment.

At the same time, we want to take full advantage in our own lives of what Buddhist teachings call our "precious human birth," a birth in which we can make choices about how we will spend our limited time on earth. The first six keys to conscious living represent choices that support *growing* up emotionally and psychologically, as well as *waking* up spiritually. For most people who are willing to make the commitment, the process is a gradual transition that takes place over many years.

One senior nun described her observations of this process, and I find her description redolent of both growing up and waking up:

> When I look at the older sisters, what I most admire
> is their good hearts. They still serve and work and
> pray and teach like they did years ago as young girls,
> but now there's a different beauty about them.
> Then they were full of ardor, wanting to become
> virtuous and worthy of God, waiting to find some-
> thing special in this holy life. Now we pray because
> we have come to love prayer; we teach or work with
> a simple natural kindness and love. It has become
> a way of giving God's joy.[2]

Imagine how sweet it would feel to wake up in the morning and know in your heart of hearts that your reason for being is to be a living instrument of love, joy, and kindness. Imagine, too, the happiness you would experience if you had gradually cultivated the wisdom to fulfill this purpose in a creative, skillful, and effective manner. I don't see these thoughts as unrealistic or Pollyanna-ish. Rather I see them as an accurate description of an organic ripening process that sincere spiritual practitioners of all stripes gradually embody over time.

One way I've noticed this ripening in my own life is in terms of how I relate to questions and answers. When I initially became aware of what's possible for us as human beings, I was in my early twenties and expressing an in-the-world, male version of the lives of the young nuns just mentioned. I was thrilled to know that there were time-tested methods of transformation that could help me move through and beyond the difficult moods and emotions that seemed to plague my life much of the time. An intense yearning for answers motivated my initial steps on the spiritual path.

In retrospect, I can see the beliefs that supported my perspective: *If I have more answers, I'll have more control. I'll feel less vulnerable, more stable, and better able to cope with the challenges life presents. I might even discover what it's like to be truly content.* While this way of thinking was a natural outgrowth of our society's emphasis on the rational mind, it served me for only a few brief years before I realized it was an entirely inadequate vision of awakening. Such a control-oriented approach left little space for the deeper mysteries of life.

As I continued to practice meditation, study perennial wisdom teachings, and engage in service work, I noticed that I was able to find answers to some of my questions and not others. Sometimes I struggled long and hard with a conundrum, got nowhere, and felt quite disheartened. Other times, the difficult issue seemed to gradually move to the background, becoming less urgent or even irrelevant. Inevitably, when that happened, a new question emerged in awareness, reflecting an ongoing process of internal reshuffling that seemed built into the nature of consciousness itself. I was too young at that point to understand the relationship between the *content* of the mind and the *processes* of the mind.

What I eventually realized is that the passing years were wearing away my attachment to certainty, control, and predictability. Like water on stone, life continually reminded me that impermanence was the way of all things and that it sometimes generated anxiety. It was pointless to resist or resent this fact of life, just as it was useless to obsess about questions I was unable to answer.

A breakthrough occurred when I recognized that something deep inside me had changed in a most welcome way. I began to embrace and appreciate the questions themselves, in the way the poet Rainer Maria Rilke talked about when he said to love the questions "like locked rooms and like books that are now written in a very foreign tongue." It was such a delightful relief to discover that "living the questions" heightened my sense of connection to both myself and other human beings who often shared the same doubts, concerns, and musings. I began to understand what Rilke meant when he went on to say, "Live the questions now."[3]

The poet is talking about the same *now* that the Dalai

Lama joyfully proclaimed when he was asked to pinpoint the happiest moment in his life. It's the only moment in which we can ever know true joy and well-being, what Buddhist teachings call "abiding happiness" or, in some translations, "enduring happiness." This is one of the great "open secrets" of profound spiritual realization. To experience abiding happiness, we have to arrive at a radically different understanding of what happiness is than the one we learned from our modern Western culture. Indeed, it is usually in the latter half of life that we have the opportunity to explore happiness in a much deeper and more nuanced light than our younger selves would have thought possible.

CONVENTIONAL HAPPINESS AND ABIDING HAPPINESS

Consider the following story from the writing of Tibetan Buddhist teacher and scholar Matthieu Ricard:

> [There is] a man I have known for twenty years who lives in the Bumthang province at the heart of the Himalayan kingdom of Bhutan. He was born without arms or legs, and he lives on the outskirts of a village in a little bamboo hut of just a few square yards. He never goes out and barely moves from the mattress on the floor. He came from Tibet forty years ago, carried by fellow refugees, and has lived in this hut ever since. The mere fact that he is still alive is extraordinary in itself, but even more strik-

ing is the joy that radiates from him. Every time I see him, he is in the same serene, simple, gentle, and unaffected frame of mind. When we bring him small gifts of food, blankets, a portable radio, he says that there was no need to bring him anything. "What could I possibly need?" he laughs.

There is usually somebody from the village to be found in his cabin—a child, an elder, a man or woman who has brought him water, some gossip. Most of all, they say, they come because it does them good to spend a little time in his company. They ask his advice. When a problem arises in the village, they usually come to him to solve it.[4]

Admittedly, this is an extreme example, perhaps too extreme for some of us to relate to. At the same time, it illustrates an important point. In conventional use, the word *happiness* refers to an emotional state of gladness or well-being that is associated with a specific set of conditions. If I get the job I really want; if I meet the mate I've been yearning for; if the result of my biopsy is negative; if I savor a beautiful sunset; if I listen to an uplifting concert by a world-class symphony orchestra or my favorite rock band; if I taste delicious, healthy food—then I feel happy. This is one kind of happiness, and it's a delight when we experience it. Sometimes this kind of happiness is the result of pleasant sense experiences. Other times, it's the result of getting what we want or not getting what we don't want, as in the case of the biopsy.

This type of happiness includes what's been called "the joy of concentration."[5] When you focus in a clear, undistracted way on whatever you're experiencing, the mind and body synchronize and become unified. This can occur during any activity, such as playing tennis, performing surgery, reading a good book, working in your garden, or watching a movie you find electrifying. It feels as if you merge into and become one with what's happening, and for a period of time your sense of subject and object collapse into pure presence, into Being. People generally don't even know this is happening until after their attention wanders, and they realize they had temporarily escaped the ego-identity that so often feels like solitary confinement. Western psychology refers to this kind of experience as a state of "flow."[6]

What these examples of conventional happiness have in common is the fact that they are all dependent on specific conditions. If I get the job offer and find out the salary is much lower than I expected it to be, my happiness might decrease significantly or disappear entirely. If I start dating the person I recently met and it turns out my initial impression was largely a projection of my own needs, I might feel painfully disillusioned and confused. If the negative biopsy means I still have problematic symptoms and don't know what's causing them, I might have to go through a difficult battery of new medical tests and a period of frightening uncertainty. If the mountain viewpoint I've chosen is in an area that is filled with biting black flies, it may feel impossible to enjoy the magic of the sunset.

Conventional happiness is quite enjoyable when it's

wisely understood, which means that it's seen clearly as what it actually is. Because it depends on specific circumstances, it is temporary and fragile by nature. If we cling to it and hope that it will remain as it is, we set ourselves up for suffering. If we learn to "hold on tightly, let go lightly," as I heard Ram Dass say many times, we appreciate the delight when it's present and gently release it when there's a change. Just as we watch the meditative mind find the felt sensation of the breath, then become distracted, and then return once again to the object of attention, we notice the arising and passing of joyful mind states over the course of the day.

Abiding happiness, in contrast, is characterized by the "happiness for no reason" I mentioned in chapter 2. This is what allows us to celebrate our journey regardless of the circumstance we're experiencing. What makes this possible is a radical shift in our understanding and experience of well-being. We come to see that there's another kind of happiness, another dimension of joy, that is *inherent in awareness itself.* It doesn't require specific conditions, and it gradually becomes a foundational part of our being. In that way, it is like a flowing underground stream that is always present and quietly exerting its influence. This innate human capacity, although only partially developed in most people, allows us to make sense of a fellow human being like the man in the hut in Bhutan. It's this kind of joy the Buddha was talking about in this well-known passage from the *Dhammapada*, or "the sayings of the Buddha":

Live in joy,
In love,
Even among those who hate.

Live in joy,
In health,
Even among the afflicted.

Live in joy,
In peace,
Even among the troubled.

. . .

Look within.
Be still.
Free from fear and attachment,
Know the sweet joy of the way.[7]

We can get a glimpse of this process in the writing of Polly Francis, a fashion illustrator and photographer who died in 1978 at the age of ninety-four. She wrote a series of essays for the *Washington Post* when she was in her nineties, and in one of them she beautifully captured the primary flavor of her inner life:

A new set of faculties seems to be coming into operation. I seem to be awakening to a larger world of wonderment—to catch little glimpses of the immensity and diversity of creation. More than at any other time in my life, I seem to be aware of the beauties of our spinning planet and the sky above.

And now I have the time to enjoy them. I feel that
old age sharpens our awareness.[8]

What we see in her words is another of the open secrets
of the spiritual path. A central task of the journey is to cultivate insight into the paradox of being and becoming. These
two interwoven aspects of experience play a central role,
consciously or unconsciously, in every human life. There's
a strong tendency in the first half of our lives to emphasize
the process of becoming. Even if we intellectually understand the relationship between these two aspects of life,
we're often so deeply conditioned by modern society that
striving becomes our dominant mode of living. Our sub-
jective experience is frequently one of lack, feeling like
we don't have any or enough of whatever we believe will
bring us fulfillment.[9] When we live this way, true happiness
becomes a receding horizon we feel we're always struggling
to reach and yet never able to actualize in a lasting or meaningful way.

The spiritual teacher Wayne Muller describes a participant in one of his workshops who was stunned when she
realized how long she'd been "seeking" and how unconsciously she'd been guided by a mindset that had, itself,
become a powerful impediment to her fulfillment.

A woman at a retreat shared how she had devoted
her whole life to spiritual seeking. She had traveled
to sacred sites, attended countless retreats and
workshops, sought teachers and guides. It had, she

confessed, been a time of much striving; it had been fruitful in some ways, yet she felt tired, weary. She was getting older. She wondered how much stamina she had left to continue her search.

"You have been a seeker for so long," I said. "Why not become a finder? At this stage in your life, what if you imagined you were ready to let go of seeking, and begin finding?" She remained silent for a long time, a look of deep confusion on her face, her head slightly tilted, as if she were trying to hear a sound far away. Then, suddenly, a laugh exploded from deep in her belly. A finder! What a delight! How could she have never imagined it before? She had always been so focused on the search, she had never taken time to rejoice in the blessing, the gift of finding.[10]

When I imagine this woman being a "finder" with the same level of commitment she demonstrated as a seeker, what comes to mind is a description of the enlightenment experience of Teijitsu, an eighteenth-century abbess of Hakujuan, a Buddhist nunnery in Japan:

She saw that arising arose, abided, fell away. She saw that knowing this arose, abided, fell away. Then she knew there was nothing more than the cane she held. Nothing to lean upon at all, and no one leaning, and she opened the clenched fist of her mind and let go and fell into the midst of everything.[11]

Embracing Paradox

When we look at the lives of people who have grown substantially in a conscious, life-affirming manner, it becomes increasingly apparent that one of the best yardsticks for assessing spiritual maturity is our capacity for embracing paradox and contradiction. We've just considered one example of the many pairs of seeming opposites that life calls on us to reconcile, being and becoming. We've also examined seeking and finding, which is one particular expression of the general concept of being and becoming.

Those who have truly ripened in the spiritual life become playfully intimate with various paradoxes and deeply curious about what we can learn from them. Indeed, once we understand the principles involved, we see paradoxes with increasing frequency. We move from either-or thinking to both-and thinking, from a largely rational, intellectual perspective to a primarily intuitive, insight-oriented perspective. For example, when seeking leads us to discover the true nature of the seeker and the nondual aspect of the ultimate mystery, there's no longer a distinction between seeking and finding. There may be times when one or the other takes precedence in the course of living; however, the basic illusion of separateness is no longer maintained. We sometimes experience ourselves as subject relating to object and other times as subject being one with object. With this in mind, let's revisit the poem mentioned in chapter 3 by the Chinese poet Li Po, who beautifully captured this multilevel understanding of reality in words.

The birds have vanished into the sky,
and now the last cloud drains away.

We sit together, the mountain and me,
until only the mountain remains.[12]

What are some of the other apparent opposites that we learn to investigate, appreciate, and celebrate as we penetrate more deeply into what Zen teachings call the Great Way? Here are some that I've explored in my own life:

work—play
sacred—profane
good—evil
joy—sorrow
self—other
persona—shadow
us—them
gain—loss
pleasure—pain
free will—determinism
praise—blame
being—doing
life—death

Huston Smith, the respected religious scholar and educator, offered a testament to this process of reconciling opposites in his autobiography, *Tales of Wonder*:

The older I get, the more the boundary between me and not-me thins and becomes transparent. I look back upon the paths I have traveled and think, This is me. I look across the table at Kendra, my wife of sixty-five years, and think, This is me. I feel my hip replacement and think, This is me. The childish *oneself versus other* becomes the mature *oneself and other* becomes, finally, *oneself as other*.[13]

In this part of the journey, we often circle back to the experience of mystery—the first of the seven keys, which played such an important role when we were setting out in the first place. Rather than desperately searching for answers, we now understand that the open heart can fully embrace what the thinking mind finds ungraspable. It's become clear to us that life is an adventure to be savored, celebrated, and surrendered to rather than an endless jig-saw puzzle with too little time to complete. Now we're free to explore our inner lives and the external world with loving curiosity and heartfelt compassion. There's nothing left to prove, and there's nobody to impress. We've learned to recognize our mistakes as stepping-stones and our successes as blessings. Since the journey of awakening ultimately has no end, we take refuge in a truth that's been with us all along yet was too obvious to see. The process is *it*. This moment is *it*. I strongly suspect it was a version of this realization that led T. S. Eliot to pen these oft-repeated words:

> We shall not cease from exploration
> And the end of all our exploring
> Will be to arrive where we started
> And know the place for the first time.[14]

This seventh key is one that gradually and subtly suffuses our lives as we live day to day, month to month, decade to decade. I once heard it described as a process of "marination." The style of celebrating the journey varies from personality to personality, situation to situation, moment to moment. The recovery of our sense of wonder is the essential common ingredient that unites all those who tread this part of the sacred path.

Our celebration of the journey now involves appreciating the paradoxes and contradictions of life and making the present moment our reference point for what's true. It bears the fruit of cultivating self-compassion *and* compassion for others. Perhaps its foremost aspect is the joy of loving "what is," whether it be pleasant or unpleasant. In the midst of this celebration, it's natural for us to further develop our intuitive wisdom and serve joyfully from the heart. We come to see that it's all part of being fully human. For reasons we may never fully understand, we are privileged to live on this fragile and beautiful earth with countless others who share in the timeless mystery that is the source, path, and goal of human life.

I want to strongly emphasize that the stage of spiritual unfolding I'm calling "celebrating the journey" is not limited to world-renowned teachers like the Dalai Lama or to "special people" who are somehow gifted in a way that most of us are not. Rather, the capacities to love unselfishly, to celebrate life just as it is, and to savor the ordinariness of our lives with a deep sense of gratitude are innate. We have all had this potential since the day we were born.

I recognized and admired this quality of celebration in Gordon McKeeman, the mentor and friend I mentioned in chapter 3, who taught me about what he called our "impulse toward wholeness." At the 1995 General Assembly of the Unitarian Universalist Association, Gordon was one of several honorees to receive an award for fifty years of service as a minister. Instead of a conventional acceptance speech, he wrote a poem that brought home to me what was possible in my life and everyone else's.

FIFTY YEARS OF MINISTRY

Fifty years is 2600 Sundays—
    That's about 2000 sermons—
        A few memorable, most mercifully forgettable.
    Maybe 200 child dedications.
How many weddings—formal and otherwise?

So many sittings with people, grieving
    —for children killed in accidents
    —for those so cornered by their lives
        that suicide was the only way
    —for those who died "too soon" "too painfully"
        or "too late"
        remembering again and again "dust thou art . . ."

A myriad of potlucks attended—
    And so far an equal number survived.
    Newsletter columns—letters—words that fly in joy,
    In sorrow and in anger, in praise.
Money raised—millions of dollars actually.
    Money given to the church, the school, the Red Cross
    (I also gave Blood—most of it to the Red Cross)
Social problems—let's see was it 20, 200, or 2000—
    I forget.
Social problems solved—none that I can remember.

Books—bought—borrowed	1,143
Books read	27
Books told I should read	7,025

Counseling the distraught—discouraged —the
    Defeated—the down-trodden—abused and confused.
The number is in the hundreds, the effects mostly
    Imponderable.

That's at least 500 monthly meetings of the Board,
    And sometimes of the interested, concerned and
    devoted.
Thousands of miles traveled, weather
    notwithstanding.

In a few odd moments, wondering how to
    beckon people toward the Holy.

Would I do it—again?

Without a moment's hesitation![15]

One of the many blessings I've experienced in knowing wise, joyful, good-hearted elders like Gordon is the recognition that happiness for no reason is a real possibility for every one of us. The central task in the second half of life is to actualize this remarkable human potential and help others to do the same. Because each of our lives is unique, we all fulfill our ultimate purpose in our own way and in our own time. To the extent that we intentionally use the seven keys to living fully and aging well, we align our living and dying with a set of sacred principles. These will guide us home to a peace that surpasses understanding and a timeless, unconditional love that never dies.

EPILOGUE

MAHATMA GANDHI went on a pilgrimage in the Indian state of Bengal in 1947. The British had recently announced the partition of India, and there were violent riots between Hindus and Muslims in the area at the time. Although he frequently gave speeches to the public, Gandhi was keeping silence on this particular day, something he was committed to doing periodically as a spiritual practice. He was sitting on a train that was just starting to pull out of the railway station when a British reporter approached him. "Do you have a message I can take back to my people?" asked the reporter. Gandhi picked up a scrap of paper, jotted a few words on it, and handed it to him. It read: "My life is my message."[1]

The conclusion of this book is both an ending and a beginning. This is a great time to ask yourself what the message of your life has been to date and what you want it to be in the future, however short or long that may be for you. This reflection is best done with a light touch and a loving heart rather than a heavy hand of judgment. My intention throughout this book has been to highlight the amazing spiritual opportunities that the second half of life offers us all. What I've shared is one particular map and a related set of perspectives that have informed my own journey through this precious human lifetime so far.

The seven keys have served me well and have given rise to a sense of gratefulness that permeates the moments of my existence, however painful or joyful they may be. My sincere wish is that they help you to fully embrace your own goodness and beauty, to serve from your heart, and to celebrate your unique experience of Life, Part Two.

ACKNOWLEDGMENTS

Writing *Life, Part Two* has given me a fresh, exciting, and deeper understanding of the way in which my life is part of a vast, interdependent web. Just as it takes a village to raise a child, it takes a great deal of collaboration, teamwork, and goodwill to give birth to a book. I feel tremendous gratitude for the many teachers, colleagues, friends, students, clients, sangha participants, retreatants, hospice patients, Shambhala Publications staff members, and family members who have contributed to this book, some directly and some indirectly.

I feel extremely fortunate to have studied, practiced, and worked with a number of wise and compassionate spiritual teachers. Some of these relationships have been deep and personal. Others have been the result of attending retreats, workshops, and seminars, reading books, listening to recordings, watching videos, attending conferences, and from other opportunities to receive teachings. I offer a sincere bow of gratefulness to Swami Satchidananda, Ram Dass, Neem Karoli Baba, Chögyam Trungpa, Thich Nhat Hanh, Joseph Goldstein, Jack Kornfield, Sharon Salzberg,

James Baraz, Sylvia Boorstein, Gordon McKeeman, Bob Kimball, Father Thomas Keating, Reb Zalman Schacter-Shalomi, Yvonne Rand, David Loy, Roshi Joan Halifax, Frank Ostaseski, Kalu Rinpoche, Thrangu Rinpoche, Pema Chödrön, and His Holiness the Dalai Lama.

I'd like to thank the many individuals, couples, and groups who have invited me into their lives over the forty-five-plus years I've been doing people work. Whether I was wearing the hat of a psychotherapist, spiritual counselor, life coach, hospice worker, minister, Naropa University faculty member, Spiritual Eldering workshop presenter, public health development worker, or meditation teacher, I've been continually inspired and uplifted by people who have the courage to attune to their impulse toward wholeness and to act on their desire to be of service in the world.

The Buddha wisely included refuge in the sangha as one of the three refuges that spiritual practitioners have found strength and peace in for over twenty-five hundred years. My thirty-year involvement with the teachers and practitioners of the Insight Meditation Community of Colorado has been and continues to be a great blessing in that regard. I'd like to offer a particular bow of thanks to senior teachers Terry Ray and Tara-Lloyd Burton. The teaching colleagues and students I met at Naropa University during the years between 1990 and 2010 also come to mind when I reflect upon what has shaped my understanding of spiritual awakening. Thanks, also, to the fine friends and colleagues whom I trained with and came to know in the inaugural Community Dharma Leader training conducted by Spirit Rock Meditation Center. Sage-ing International, a reincarnation of the Spiritual Eldering Institute I used to work for, is an organization I recently reconnected with and a community of people who share many of the values and visions of conscious aging discussed in this book.

There are a number of people at Shambhala Publications I'd like to acknowledge. First and foremost, I'd like to express my appreciation to Matt Zepelin, my editor. Matt, your skill, patience, commitment, and level of consciousness made this a much better book than I imagined it could be when I first sat down to write it. I'd like to thank John Golebiewski for additional editorial support. I've really appreciated the bright, generous energy you consistently brought to our communications. Thanks, too, to my marketing team, Mike Henton and Tori Henson, both of whom do their work with great skill and care.

There are a number of close personal friends and family members whose love, kindness, and patience have been a source of strength and support throughout this project. I'm very grateful to a friend and patron who gifted me with the funds to take time away from other activities in order to write. Although you've asked to be anonymous, it's important to me that you know this book would not have happened without your generosity and vision. I want to mention my long-standing friendships with Ted Barrett-Page, David Loy, and Nathan Berolzheimer. Each of you contributed much more than you probably realize to helping me bring this book to completion. I thank all three of you for enabling me to experience the way joyful friendships actualize creative energy and an authentic embracing of "the ten thousand joys and the ten thousand sorrows."

My wife, Marsha, and my daughter, Laura, have supported this project from its inception. You are the brightest lights in my life, and I feel blessed to be sharing it with you. Your listening, feedback, honesty, and caring have helped me to stay on track and have provided the nourishment I needed to make the writing of this book a "path with heart" and a celebration. I love you both very much and I dedicate this book to the two of you.

NOTES

INTRODUCTION

1. Now called the Mindfulness-Based Transpersonal Counseling program.
2. Carl Jung, "The Stages of Life," in *The Collected Works of C. G. Jung*, ed. and trans. Gerhard Adler and R. F. C. Hull (Princeton, NJ: Princeton University Press, 1969), 8:87.
3. Becca R. Levy, Martin D. Slade, Suzanne R. Kunkel, and Stanislav V. Kasl, "Longevity Increased by Positive Self-Perceptions of Aging," *Journal of Personality and Social Psychology* 83, no. 2 (August 2002): 261–70.

1. EMBRACING THE MYSTERY

1. Huston Smith, *Tales of Wonder: Adventures Chasing the Divine, an Autobiography* (New York: HarperCollins, 2009), 169.
2. Thich Nhat Hanh, *Touching Peace: Practicing the Art of Mindful Living* (Berkeley, CA: Parallax Press, 1987), 1.
3. Percy Bysshe Shelley, "A Defence of Poetry," in *English Essays: Sidney to Macauley*, The Harvard Classics, vol. 27 (New York: P.F. Collier & Son, 1909–14; bartleby.com, 2009), https://www.bartleby.com/27/23.html.
4. Thich Nhat Hanh, *Present Moment Wonderful Moment* (Berkeley, CA: Parallax Press, 1990), 51.
5. Wendell Berry, *Standing by Words: Essays* (Berkeley, CA: Counterpoint, 1983), 205.
6. William Bridges, *Transitions* (New York: Lifelong Books, 2019), 4.
7. Ram Dass, *Remember—Be Here Now* (San Cristobal, NM: Lama Foundation, 1971), 97.

2. Choosing a Vision

1. Matthieu Ricard, *Happiness* (New York: Little, Brown and Company, 2003), 42.
2. Yogiraj Sri Swami Satchidananda, *Integral Yoga Hatha* (New York: Holt, Rinehart, and Winston, 1970), xvii.
3. John Welwood, *Perfect Love, Imperfect Relationships: Healing the Wound of the Heart* (Boston: Trumpeter Books, 2006), 4.
4. Stephen Mitchell, ed., *The Enlightened Heart* (New York: Harper Perennial, 1989), 5.
5. Edward W. Desmonde, "A Pencil in the Hand of God," *Time*, December 4, 1989, 48.
6. Jack Kornfield, "Bodhisattva Vows," accessed April 20, 2021, www.jackkornfield.com/bodhisattva-vows.
7. Bruce W. Heinemann, *The Nature of Wisdom* (New York: Barnes & Noble, 2007), 68.

3. Awakening Intuition

1. See 1 Kings 19:11–12.
2. Ram Dass and Paul Gorman, *How Can I Help?* (New York: Alfred A. Knopf, 1985), 110.
3. Guy Armstrong, *Emptiness* (Somerville, MA: Wisdom Publications, 2017,) 6–7.
4. Stephen Mitchell, ed., *The Enlightened Heart* (New York: HarperCollins, 1989), 32.
5. Ram Dass, "The Paradox of Involvement vs. Non-attachment," Love, Serve, Remember Foundation, accessed April 20, 2021, www.ramdass.org/paradox-involvement-vs-non-attachment/.
6. Ram Dass, *Changing Lenses* (Los Angeles: Love, Serve, Remember Foundation, 2018), 47.
7. Martha Crampton, *Guidelines for Testing the Authenticity of Intuition* (Montreal: Canadian Institute of Psychosynthesis, 1974).
8. Stephen Mitchell, *Tao Te Ching* (New York: HarperCollins, 1988), 15.
9. Antoine de Saint-Exupéry, *The Little Prince*, trans. Richard Howard (Orlando, FL: Harcourt, Inc., 2000), 63.
10. Jim Fallon, personal e-mail with author, November 6, 2019.

4. Committing to Inner Work

1. James Joyce, "A Painful Case," in *Dubliners* (London: Jonathan Cape, 1954).
2. *The Spiritual Eldering Workbook* (Boulder, CO: The Spiritual Eldering Institute, 1996), 47.
3. Ram Dass and Paul Gorman, *How Can I Help?* (New York: Alfred A. Knopf, 1985), 116–17.
4. Jack Kornfield, *A Path with Heart* (New York: Bantam Books, 1993), 108.
5. Robert Bly, *The Kabir Book* (Boston: Beacon Press, 1971), 37.
6. Meister Eckhart, "Some of Eckhart's Sayings," The Eckhart Society, accessed May 10, 2021, www.eckhartsociety.org/eckhart/some-eck harts-sayings.
7. Andrew Harvey and Michael Toms, "Of Rumi and Apocalypse," Program Number 2451, New Dimensions Radio, accessed May 10, 2021, https://programs.newdimensions.org/search?type=pro duct&q=program+2451.
8. Joan Halifax, *Being with Dying* (Boston: Shambhala Publications, 2008), 192.
9. Abraham Maslow, *Toward a Psychology of Being* (Floyd, VA: Sublime Books, 2014), 30.
10. Sharon Salzberg, *Faith: Trusting Your Own Deepest Experience* (New York: Riverhead Books, 2002).

5. Suffering Effectively

1. Shinzen Young, "Learning to Suffer More Effectively," Awakin, accessed April 21, 2021, www.awakin.org/read/view.php?tid=705.
2. Charlotte Joko Beck, *Ordinary Wonder: Zen Life and Practice* (Boulder, CO: Shambhala Publications, 2021), 23.
3. Mary Karr, *The Liars' Club* (New York: Viking Penguin, 1995), xvi.
4. Rachel Naomi Remen, *Kitchen Table Wisdom* (New York: Riverhead Books, 1996), 75.
5. Nyanaponika Thera and Bhikku Bodhi, trans. *Numerical Discourses of the Buddha: An Anthology of Suttas from the Anguttara Nikaya* (Lanham, MD: Altamira Press, 1999), 135.
6. "Hollywood Superstar Who Expanded Her Acting Range," *Irish Times*, accessed May 8, 2021, https://www.irishtimes.com/news /hollywood-superstar-who-expanded-her-acting-range-1.1004898.

7. Aleksandr Solzhenitsyn, "Growing Old," quoted in David Remnick, "Deep in the Woods," Letter from Moscow, *New Yorker*, July 29, 2001, www.newyorker.com/magazine/2001/08/06/deep-in-the-woods.

8. Personal communication with author, April 7, 2017.

6. SERVING FROM THE HEART

1. John Stevens, trans., *One Robe, One Bowl* (New York: Weatherhill, Inc., 1975), 75.

2. Seva Foundation, "The Waldenwoods Statement," founding meeting, Waldenwoods, MI, December 1978.

3. Jack Canfield and Mark Victor Hanson, *A 3rd Serving of Chicken Soup for the Soul* (Deerfield Beach, FL: Health Communications, Inc., 1996), 70.

4. *Quickening—Newsletter of the American College of Nurse Midwives*, March/April 2005.

5. Quoted in Koun Franz, "Here I Am," *Nyohō Zen* (blog), https://nyoho.com/2013/04/01/here-i-am.

6. Stuart Hample and Eric Marshall, *Children's Letters to God* (New York: Workman Publishing Co., 1991), 95.

7. Quoted in Frances Vaughan, *Awakening Intuition* (New York: Doubleday, 1979), 72.

8. Mark Nepo, *The Exquisite Risk: Daring to Live an Authentic Life* (New York: Three Rivers Press, 2005), 5.

9. National Public Radio, *Morning Edition*, March 28, 2008, https://storycorps.org/stories/julio-diaz.

10. Anne Lamott, "Have a Little Faith," *AARP Magazine*, December 2014 / January 2015, 57.

11. Richard Selzer as quoted in Jack Kornfield, *The Art of Forgiveness, Lovingkindness, and Peace* (New York: Bantam, 2002), 110–11.

12. James Baraz, personal e-mail with author, June 15, 2013.

13. Philip Pullella, "Pope Tacks Sign on His Apartment Door: 'No Whining,'" Reuters, July 14, 2017, www.reuters.com/article /us-pope-sign-idUSKBN19Z0XW.

14. Evelyn Einstein and Alice Calaprice, *Dear Professor Einstein: Albert Einstein's Letters to and from Children* (New York: Barnes and Noble Press, 2002), 184.

7. CELEBRATING THE JOURNEY

1. Matthieu Ricard, "The Happiest Day in Your Life," *Matthieu Ricard* (blog), December 21, 2011, www.matthieuricard.org/en/blog/posts/the-happiest-day-in-your-life.

2. Quoted in Jack Kornfield, *After the Ecstasy, the Laundry* (New York: Bantam Books, 2000), 290–91.

3. Rainer Maria Rilke, *Letters to a Young Poet* (Novato, CA: New World Library, 2000), 31.

4. Matthieu Ricard, *Happiness: A Guide to Developing Life's Most Important Skill* (New York: Little, Brown and Company, 2007), 77.

5. Joseph Goldstein, *The Experience of Insight* (Santa Cruz, CA: Unity Press, 1976), 108.

6. Mihaly Csikszentmihalyi, *Flow: The Psychology of Optimal Experience* (New York: Harper Perennial, 2008), xi.

7. Thomas Byrom, trans., *Dhammapada: The Sayings of the Buddha* (Boston: Shambhala Publications, 1993), 54–55.

8. Polly Francis as quoted in Drew Leder, *Spiritual Passages* (New York: Jeremy P. Tarcher/Putnam, 1997), 144.

9. For an interesting analysis of this topic, see David Loy, *Lack and Transcendence* (Somerville, MA: Wisdom Publications, 2018), 31–32.

10. Wayne Muller, *Sabbath: Finding Rest, Renewal, and Delight in Our Busy Lives* (New York: Bantam Books, 1999), 202.

11. Sallie Tisdale, *Women of the Way: Discovering 2,500 Years of Buddhist Wisdom* (New York: HarperCollins, 2006), 263.

12. Stephen Mitchell, ed., *The Enlightened Heart: An Anthology of Sacred Poetry* (New York: Harper Perennial, 1989), 32.

13. Huston Smith, *Tales of Wonder* (New York: HarperOne, 2009), 187.

14. T. S. Eliot, "Little Gidding," no. 4 of *Four Quartets*, accessed April 21, 2021, http://www.paikassociates.com/pdf/fourquartets.pdf.

15. Gordon McKeeman, "Fifty Years of Ministry," *Elderberries: Newsletter of the Unitarian Universalist Retired Ministers and Partners Association*, August 1995.

EPILOGUE

1. Jaydev Jana, "The Lonely Pilgrimage," The Statesman, April 23, 2021, www.thestatesman.com/opinion/the-lonely-pilgrimage-1502867168.html.

CREDITS

ABOUT THE AUTHOR

DAVID CHERNIKOFF , M.S.W., M.DIV., began the study and
practice of meditation in 1971 and started teaching insight
meditation in 1988. He trained as a yoga teacher at the Integral Yoga Institute and completed the inaugural Community
Dharma Leader program at Spirit Rock Meditation Center.
His teaching has been heavily influenced by Jack Kornfield,
Sharon Salzberg, Joseph Goldstein and other teachers associated with the Insight Meditation Society and Spirit Rock.
David also trained with Tibetan teachers during a three-
year stay in Nepal and with Zen teacher Yvonne Rand. His
interest in end-of-life care led him to work at the Hanuman
Foundation Dying Center in Santa Fe and then to direct the
Mesilla Valley Hospice in Las Cruces, New Mexico.

As someone with a longtime interest in interspiritual dialogue, David has also studied and practiced with spiritual guides from diverse contemplative traditions, most notably Ram Dass, Father Thomas Keating, and Rabbi Zalman Schachter-Shalomi.

David taught psychology and meditation at Naropa University for many years and worked as the education and training director of the Spiritual Eldering Institute, a conscious aging program later renamed Sage-ing International. Currently he is one of the guiding teachers of the Insight Meditation Community of Colorado and has a private practice as a spiritual counselor and life coach in Boulder, Colorado. He teaches workshops and retreats throughout the U.S.

For more information, visit www.davidchernikoff.com.